LITTLE BOOK OF
TITANIC

LITTLE BOOK OF
TITANIC

First published in the UK in 2011

© G2 Entertainment Limited 2011

www.G2ent.co.uk

Printed and bound printed in the EU

ISBN 978-1-907803-00-0

Contents

Introduction

▼ A scene from the film *A Night to Remember*.

It is approaching 100 years since the 'practically unsinkable' White Star liner *Titanic* sank beneath the waves and into the history books. In the years that followed that night in April 1912 much has been written about the ship and the tragic loss of life that occurred following its collision with an iceberg

▼ A scene from the film *A Night to Remember*.

during its maiden voyage to New York, but still the *Titanic* continues to fascinate. In film, too, the story of the sinking has been told or reinterpreted – from *A Night to Remember*, based on Walter Lord's pioneering history of the sinking, through Sir Lew Grade's costly film of Clive Cussler's bestselling novel, *Raise the Titanic*, to James Cameron's blockbuster *Titanic* starring Kate Winslet and Leonardo DiCaprio.

For more than 70 years the wreck of the *Titanic* lay undisturbed, but with its discovery, a whole new industry has been spawned with film crews recording the ship's remains and tours down to view it. Artefacts removed from the debris field have been exhibited and concern over the wreck's condition has led to legal action over its actual ownership. Such has been the activity over the 25 years since its discovery that the wreck's condition has deteriorated rapidly and it may well completely disintegrate by the end of the current century.

The fascination with the sinking of the *Titanic* is easy to explain. The loss of such a prestigious ship on its maiden voyage was bound to cause interest, particularly as the passenger list included many of the era's rich and famous, leading to rumours that the ship was conveying a veritable treasure trove of wealth. There was the drama of the actual sinking itself, the band playing on as the ship slid under the waves and the failure of the crew to fully utilise the admittedly inadequate lifeboat provision. There were tales of heroism, such as the engineering crew who died trying to keep the pumps and generators going but whose action probably delayed the sinking for over an hour, allowing the lifeboats to get away, and of those employed in the wireless room who stuck to their posts as long as possible trying to summon assistance to the stricken vessel.

This book provides an overview of the history of the sinking of the *Titanic* and of its aftermath.

▲ Action from the James Cameron film *Titanic*.

The Latest, Largest and Finest Steamer Afloat

Competition between shipping lines was fierce during the last decade of the 19th century, and profits for the shipping companies involved were limited. In 1893 during a crossing of the Atlantic, the notable financier John Pierpont Morgan, who had interests in banking, railways and steel, was asked whether it was practical to try to buy up shipping lines in order to reduce competition and so encourage more realistic (and profitable) fares. Morgan thought that it ought to be, but it was not until later in the decade that he started to put this policy into practice when he acquired American Inman and Red Star lines.

In 1902 Morgan created the International Mercantile Marine Company (IMM) with the idea that competition on the all-important transatlantic route could be reduced through co-operation and thus profitability enhanced; IMM's route to co-operation was to buy up competitors.

Morgan bought into a number of shipping lines, including Atlantic Transport, Leyland and Dominion, before turning his attention to the larger British-owned companies, Cunard and White Star. After a bitter battle Morgan acquired White Star Line for £10 million, making former White Star Line managing director J Bruce Ismay chairman and managing director of IMM in early 1904. However, the Cunard deal was thwarted by the British government offering Cunard a soft loan that allowed the line to construct the *Lusitania* and *Mauretania*, and also providing £150,000 per annum as part of the mail contract. The scene was set for the development and construction of the 'Olympic' class of liner in order to compete with the new ships under construction for Cunard.

Cunard's new liners, both entering service in 1906, had been built for speed in an effort to claim the 'Blue Riband' title for the fastest crossing of the North Atlantic, but there was a price to be paid for speed. Each additional knot required ever increasing amounts of coal and this added both to weight and cost. In looking towards *Olympic* and her sister vessels *Titanic* and *Britannic*, White Star Line decided against competing on speed but in favour of providing the greater luxury. Of the three, only the *Olympic* ever completed a commercial sailing, with *Titanic* being sunk on her maiden voyage and *Britannic*, converted for use as a hospital ship, being sunk in the Aegean Sea before she could enter

◀ The *Titanic* under construction in the Arrol Gantry at the Harland & Wolff shipyard, Belfast.

▼ The *Titanic* in dry dock, February 1912.

commercial service following a mine strike during World War I.

Work was not yet complete on the *Olympic* when the keel of the *Titanic* was laid down in the Belfast shipyard of Harland & Wolff on 31 March 1909 as yard (ship) No 401 with hull No 390904. At 882ft 9in in length, the second in the Olympic class was six inches longer than the *Olympic*, but had an identical beam of 92ft 6in and a draught of 34ft 7in. The *Titanic* had a Gross Registered Tonnage (GRT) of 46,238 tons and a displacement of 52,310 tons.

She was fitted with two reciprocating four-cylinder, triple expansion steam engines to turn the two bronze triple-blade side propellers, and a single low-pressure Parsons turbine for the bronze four-blade central propeller. The engines that powered the three propellers were fed by 25 double-ended and four single-ended Scotch-type boilers, rated at 215psi, fired by 159 coal-burning furnaces. In all, the engines provided enough power to achieve a maximum speed of 23.75 knots with a service speed of 21 knots.

The ship was constructed with a double hull, designed to accommodate water for use in the boilers and additional water to provide ballast (hence stability) whilst at sea. The ship was, however, designed and built with only a single-skin hull.

Three of the ship's four funnels were used to exhaust smoke and fumes from the engine room, whilst the fourth provided ventilation for the engine room and the air required to keep the fires in the furnaces alight. Thus, steam and smoke should only ever have been seen emerging from the leading three funnels; images that show smoke emerging from the fourth are incorrect.

Following the laying down of the keel, work proceeded rapidly on ship No 401, with the ship being launched shortly after noon on 31 May 1911 watched by an estimated crowd of some 100,000. On top of the gantry above the ship flew the Union Flag on one side and the Stars and Stripes on the other, with the White Star Line's red pennant flying in the middle. Below, a line of signal flags proclaimed the message 'SUCCESS'.

With the *Olympic* now completed, the Harland & Wolff yard could turn its attention towards the final completion of the *Titanic* with a view to the ship's maiden voyage beginning on 20 March 1912. However, two incidents to the *Olympic* – the collision with HMS *Hawke* and the loss of a propeller – required the ship to return twice to Belfast for repair. On the first return it became evident that the repair work required would cause serious delays to the completion of the *Titanic* and, on 10 October 1911, it was announced that the new ship's maiden voyage would now begin on Wednesday 10 April 1912.

As the *Titanic*, along with her sister ships, had been designed for luxury and not primarily for speed, she was opulently fitted out to a standard that far exceeded that of any other liner then

▼ The *Titanic* being guided down Belfast Lough by the tugs *Hercules*, *Huskisson*, *Herculaneum* and *Hornby*.

in service. She was provided with a squash court, separate libraries for all three classes of passenger, a Turkish bath, gymnasium and swimming pool. The first class rooms, in particular, were lavishly fitted out; the smoking room, for example, was provided with an old rose carpet and pink drapes over the curtains.

However, the *Titanic* was unusual in that it offered reasonable facilities for third class passengers in an era when this class of passenger was generally poorly provided for. Apart from the third class library, there was also a smoking room, two bars and a general room for the use of third class passengers. This was panelled and framed in pine with

◀ A replica of the first class hall on the *Titanic*.

▼ The *Titanic* had many first class suites as seen in this replica.

a white enamel finish. The chairs in the room were made of teak and there was a separate adjacent smoking room for the men, furnished in teak but panelled and framed in oak. Third class sleeping accommodation – designed for 1,026 passengers – was located on the front section of deck D and on fore and aft sections of decks E and F. The distance between the fore and aft sections meant that the crew was able to segregate unmarried emigrants by sex. Amongst the accommodation provided for single men were 164 'open berths' (bunks in a dormitory).

Second class rooms were on B and C decks. The smoking room was panelled in oak with oak furniture upholstered in dark green morocco leather. On C deck, the second class library was panelled in sycamore, with mahogany furniture covered in tapestries and with green silk drapes in the windows. The quality of the second class public rooms was of a standard comparable to first class on many of the competing liners.

The first class dining room, with seating for 532, was situated on deck D,

LITTLE BOOK OF **TITANIC**

and was the largest single room on board the ship. The second class dining room offered accommodation for 394 and the two third class saloons, located on deck F, could accommodate a total of 473.

The most sumptuous part of the ship's interior was the forward first class staircase. This was located between the first and second funnels and extended down as far as E deck. Decorated with gilded balustrades and fitted with oak panelling, it was topped by an ornate dome made out of wrought iron and glass. On the uppermost landing was a large panel containing a clock supported by the allegorical figures of Glory and Honour. A second, but less ornate, staircase was located between the third and fourth funnels; this was again surmounted by a glass and wrought iron dome.

The captain's quarters were located on the boat deck on the starboard side just aft of the wheelhouse (which stood behind the bridge). The other deck officers had their cabins in the same section; this area, known as the 'officers' house', was built around the foremost funnel. The majority of crew members were allocated bunks on decks D, E, F and G.

◀ The magnificent dome-covered grand staircase as depicted in this replica.

▶ An advertisement for the *Titanic*, showing some of her facilities.

▶▶ The gymnasium ably demonstrated by the ship's gymnast TW McCawley.

The ship was also technologically advanced for its time. Three lifts were provided: two were for the use of first class passengers but, again unusually for the period, a third was provided for second class travellers. Making use of steam-powered generators, the ship was also fully fitted with electric lighting, but not with a public address system, which would have been of particular use on the night of the disaster. In order to contact other vessels and land, when in range, the ship was provided with two Marconi wireless sets rated at 1.5kW and each had a range of 400 miles. Whilst working the wirelesses, the radio operators could hear transmissions made to and from other ships and this would play a part before and after the collision. The wireless room was located on the boat deck on the port side towards the aft section of the officers' house.

Because of the delays caused by repairs to the *Olympic*, it was not until 10am on Tuesday 2 April 1912 that the *Titanic* was ready to start her sea trials. On board were 78 members of the 'black gang' – those required to work the engines – and 41 officers and senior crew, including Captain Edward Smith

who had boarded his new command for the first time on 1 April.

Assisted by tugs, the *Titanic* slipped its moorings and entered the Victoria Channel towards Belfast Lough at around 6am. Some miles further on, two miles offshore from Carrickfergus, the tugs were released. Captain Smith ran up the blue and white signal flag for the letter 'A' (representing 'I am undertaking sea trials') and the trials commenced. On board was the Board of Trade's surveyor in Belfast, Francis Carruthers, who had undertaken some 2,000 visits to the Harland & Wolff yard during the ship's construction. Carruthers was impressed by the ship's turning circle – 3,850 feet at 20.5 knots – and by the fact that she could make an emergency stop in 850 yards when travelling at 20 knots with the engines being thrown from 'full ahead' through 'stop' to 'full astern'.

The sea trials took a single day and at 7pm, after dropping the port and starboard anchors, the Board of Trade inspector issued a certificate of seaworthiness valid for one year from 2 April 1912. With the ship having received Board of Trade certification, she was officially handed over by Harland & Wolff to the White Star Line.

Following her sea trials, the *Titanic* headed into the Irish Sea at 8pm the same day to make the 570-mile trip to Southampton and the start of her maiden voyage. During this trip, the *Titanic* achieved 23.5 knots – the maximum speed that she'd ever attain.

▼ The *Titanic* on her sea trials in Belfast Lough.

Design Features that Contributed to the Tragedy

Although the epithet 'unsinkable' is often associated with the promotion of the White Star Line's new ship to the public and media, it is generally believed that the phrase used was 'practically unsinkable'; certainly this was the term used in the eminent contemporary trade publication *The Shipbuilder*. The ship's design included a range of features that contributed to its safety and most people could not conceive of a situation that could cause sufficient damage to sink the ship. However, there were aspects of the design that contributed to the unfolding events of 14 and 15 April 1912 and the outcome.

The ship was constructed with a double hull to accommodate water for the boilers and as ballast, but it was only single skin. One of the lessons of the sinking was that future ships were constructed with a double-skin hull.

It has been suggested that one reason for the ship's fate was the quality of steel used in its construction. Following recovery of part of the ship's hull, the steel used was subjected to detailed analysis. The tests showed that at low temperatures – and at the point the *Titanic* struck the iceberg the water temperature was just below freezing – the steel would become weaker and prone to 'brittle fracture' as a result of the higher level of sulphur in the metal. The report concluded that the real tragedy of the *Titanic* was that better construction techniques and a better quality of steel plate might have averted her loss or resulted in a slower rate of

flooding that may have saved more crew and passengers. The reality, however, was that the builders of the ship used the best quality steel available to them at the time and, whilst perhaps not up to modern standards of construction and thickness, the robustness of the hull is amply demonstrated by how well it withstood hitting the sea bed. Ultimately, the fate of the ship wasn't determined by the thickness or quality of the steel plating used, but by the inherent weakness of its design in terms of the lack of full bulkheads.

As a gesture towards safety, the *Olympic* and *Titanic* were fitted with 16 watertight compartments separated by strong bulkheads. These were divided by doors held up in the open position by electro-magnetic latches; in the event of an emergency, the doors could be closed rapidly by use of a switch on the bridge. Unfortunately, whilst these transverse bulkheads offered considerable protection, they did not extend through the full height of the ship – they extended only to 10 feet above the waterline. This meant that

▲ The single-skin hull of the *Titanic* was a major contributor to the ship's sinking.

▲ Once over the bulkheads the passenger areas of the ship were soon overcome by water as illustrated in this film still.

▶ The *Titanic* shared the same triple-screw configuration as her sister ship the *Olympic*.

once a number of compartments were compromised, water could seep over the top. Following the loss of the *Titanic*, the third vessel in the class, the *Britannic*, had her design modified to reduce this risk.

In the ship's triple-screw configuration, the two outermost propellers were powered by reciprocating steam engines, which were reversible; the central screw was driven by a steam turbine, which was not reversible. This meant that when First Officer Murdoch issued orders to reverse engines in order to avoid hitting the iceberg, he actually undermined the manoeuvrability of the vessel as the central turbine could not reverse

during the 'full steam astern' order and so simply stopped turning. In addition, the location of the central propeller directly in front of the rudder made the rudder less effective. The training procedures for the Olympic class ships laid down that the correct method for dealing with the problem would have been to switch the port propeller to full astern whilst retaining full steam ahead with the remaining two engines. This would have had the effect of making the ship turn sharply to port and thus, theoretically, pulling away from the iceberg. It is impossible to tell whether the ship would have avoided the iceberg had Murdoch adopted the correct method; conventional wisdom, however, suggests that the speed and proximity of the *Titanic* were such that the collision was inevitable.

The problem with the propellers was compounded by the design of the rudder itself. Whilst, as with the lifeboats, the provision was within the legal limits, the rudder was too small for a ship the size of the *Titanic*. The rudders fitted to the contemporary Cunard liners *Mauretania* and *Lusitania* were much bigger than that fitted to either the *Olympic* or *Titanic* – worries

over the increasing size of ships and of manoeuvring them in an emergency were not major priorities as far as White Star and Harland & Wolff were concerned.

Half of the *Titanic's* forward promenade on A deck, which was located below the boat deck, was enclosed against the outside weather. Whilst the windows could be opened in the event of fine weather, normally they were kept locked. This was to have dire consequences when the ship foundered as, when the lifeboats came to be launched, the keys for opening the windows to allow those from A deck to get to the lifeboats were absent and valuable time was lost trying to locate them.

The *Titanic* was designed to carry 3,547 people – 2,603 passengers with a crew of 944. On the maiden voyage, a total of 1,317 passengers were on board, comprising 324 first class, 285 second class and 708 third class, as well as 891 members of crew. In case of emergency, the *Titanic* was fitted with 20 lifeboats comprising 14 standard lifeboats (Nos 3-16), two emergency cutters (Nos 1 and 2) and four Engelhardt collapsible (A-D). Lifeboats on the port side were

given even numbers and those on the starboard side were given odd ones. There were also 48 or 49 cork ring lifebuoys dispersed around the ship and 3,560 canvas and cork life jackets, but most people in the water died from the effects of cold rather than by drowning.

The main lifeboats had a capacity of 980 in total and the four collapsibles provided for 196 more. The *Titanic*, therefore, was provided with lifeboat accommodation for about a third of the total number of passengers and crew on board if she was fully loaded. As this was not the case on her maiden voyage, there was theoretically lifeboat accommodation for just over half of the people on board. In fact, lifeboat provision aboard the *Titanic* exceeded the legal requirement. Under regulations introduced in 1894, a ship of 10,000 tons or more only needed to carry 16 lifeboats. The growth in the size of ships since then made these regulations woefully inadequate and, in case the Board of Trade regulations changed during the ship's construction, the *Titanic's* designers had allowed for the installation of a total of 64. It was alleged at the US Inquiry – but refuted by Harold Sanderson, the vice-president

◀ Lifeboats included standard, emergency and collapsible ones.

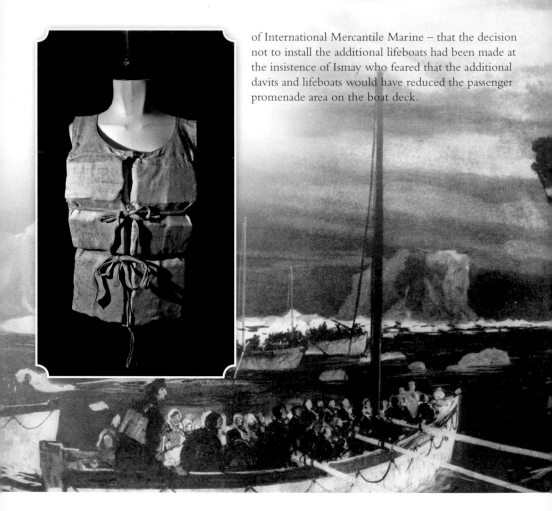

DESIGN FEATURES THAT CONTRIBUTED TO THE TRAGEDY

of International Mercantile Marine – that the decision not to install the additional lifeboats had been made at the insistence of Ismay who feared that the additional davits and lifeboats would have reduced the passenger promenade area on the boat deck.

Life on Board

The *Titanic* functioned with a crew of 892. A large number were there purely to see to the needs of the passengers. Apart from the 69 members of staff employed in the Café Parisien, there were 421 men and women in the Victualling Department, of whom 322 were stewards assigned to each class's dining saloon, public rooms, cabins and recreational facilities, and 62 were galley and kitchen staff. Also on board were two doctors and a matron to staff the ship's sick bay.

The ship's band comprised bandleader Wallace Hartley and seven other musicians. On board the ship,

the band was normally split in two: one group of three (a pianist, cellist and violinist) played in the second class dining saloon or lounge while the remaining five played for first class passengers. The former group wore blue jackets, whilst those in first class wore white jackets and blue trousers. The division was not rigid as every member of the orchestra was expected to know every song in the company's song book and recognise instantly any of the 352 tunes by its number when announced by Hartley.

The set meal times were one of the few areas where White Star laid down a rigid timetable. Breakfast was served to all classes between 8.30am and 10.30am. Luncheon for first and second class passengers and dinner for third class was served between 1pm and 2.30pm. Dinner for first and second class passengers and tea for third class was served between 6pm and 7.30pm. The Captain's Table, with seating for six, was located amidships towards the front of the room.

A vast amount of food was required to cater the 2,000-plus passengers and crew on board for the transatlantic voyage. The foodstuffs

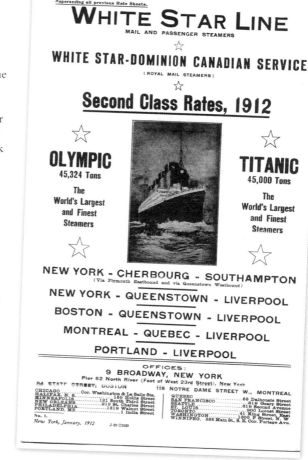

Loaded at Southampton prior to the maiden voyage included:

Fresh meat	75,000lb	Sugar	10,000lb
Fresh fish	1,000lb	Flour	250 barrels
Salted/dry fish	4,000lb	Apples	36,000
Bacon/ham	7,500lb	Oranges	36,000
Poultry/game	25,000lb	Lemons	16,000
Fresh eggs	40,000	Grapes	1,000lb
Sausages	2,500lb	Grapefruit	13,000
Potatoes	40 tons	Marmalade/jam	1,120lb
Onions	3,500lb	Fresh milk	1,500gal
Tomatoes	3,500lb	Fresh cream	2,400pt
Fresh asparagus	800 bundles	Condensed milk	600gal
Fresh green peas	2,500lb	Fresh butter	6,000lb
Lettuce	8,000 heads	Ale/stout	15,000 bottles
Sweetbreads	1,000	Wines	1,000 bottles
Ice cream	1,750qt	Minerals	1,200 bottles
Coffee	2,200lb	Cigars	8,000
Tea	800lb	Non-drinking water	664 tons
Rice/dried beans	10,000lb	Drinking (fresh) water	792 tons

Unlike other shipping companies, White Star Line's cutlery, linen and crockery was not branded with the name of the ship, making interchange between the various ships operated by the company more straightforward. The *Titanic* was provided with:

57,600 pieces of crockery including:
• 12,000 dinner plates
• 4,500 breakfast saucers
• 1,500 soufflé dishes
• 4,500 soup bowls
• 1,000 cream jugs
• 1,200 pie dishes
29,000 pieces of glassware including:
• 2,000 wine glasses
• 1,500 champagne glasses
• 300 claret jugs
44,000 items of cutlery including:
• 1,500 fish knives
• 1,500 fruit knives
• 400 toast racks
• 1,000 oyster forks
• 100 pairs of grape scissors
• 300 nutcrackers
• 400 pairs of asparagus tongs
196,100 items of linen including:
• 4,000 aprons
• 15,000 single sheets
• 45,000 table napkins
• 7,500 bath towels
• 6,500 pantry towels

First and second class ticket holders were allowed to use the à la carte restaurant on deck B. This was run under contract by Luigi Gatti with a staff drawn from his two London restaurants. If passengers elected to use the à la carte restaurant throughout the journey rather than the main dining rooms, they were offered a discount of $15–$25. The à la carte restaurant, which served hot food from 8am through to 11pm every day and which could seat 137 at 49 tables, was panelled in French walnut with a two-tone Dubarry carpet.

First class passengers were exclusively entitled to use the Café Parisien, which was located adjacent to the à la carte restaurant on deck B. The Café Parisien was also staffed by employees drawn from the two restaurants owned by Gatti in London.

The two wireless operators did not work for the White Star Line either, but were employed directly by the Marconi International Marine Communications Co Ltd. The ship was allowed to send free messages to its owners, other vessels and the shore, provided that these messages never exceeded 30 words per message. The real money

as far as Marconi was concerned came from relaying messages to and from passengers.

The *Titanic* was a designated Royal Mail Ship (RMS) and part of her planned role was to ship mail to and from North America. She had 3,364 mail bags on board. The sea Post Office service offered postal authorities an opportunity to process the mail during the ship's passage, and it offered the White Star Line a reliable and predictable source of income. On board *Titanic* was a state of the art sorting office and mail room where five postal workers, employed by the New York and Southampton branches of the sea Post Office, sorted and cancelled the mail en route to the ship's destination as well as dealing with any letters which were posted on board by passengers and crew.

Whilst the ship headed westwards, the *Titanic*'s passengers enjoyed the facilities that the ship offered. Apart from the orchestra, the crew did not lay on activities for the passengers in the belief that the ship was well provided with entertainment options. Thus, it would have been possible to see passengers reading books in the libraries, making use of the swimming pool,

gymnasium and Turkish baths, playing cards, walking on the promenade deck and playing deck games.

Life was not so comfortable for some members of the crew. Amongst others, the engineering crew consisted of 73 trimmers who moved coal to the furnaces, 176 firemen who kept the furnaces fed with coal, 25 engineers responsible for keeping the engines, generators, and other mechanical

equipment running, 10 electricians and 30 greasers who maintained the machinery in the engine room. The heat in the boiler rooms usually exceeded 120°F (49°C) and most of the firemen worked wearing only their undershirts and shorts. The coal trimmers worked inside the coal bunkers, which were poorly lit, full of coal dust and extremely hot from the residual heat that rose up into them from the boilers.

The Ship's Crew

▼ Joseph Boxhall.

Joseph Boxhall – On hearing the look-out bell on the night of the disaster Fourth Officer Boxhall (aged 28) headed for the bridge and was ordered by Captain Smith to inspect the forward section of the ship. He later calculated the position of the ship for inclusion within the distress signal. He was one of those who believed he saw masthead lights from a nearby ship (often believed to be the SS *Californian*). Boxhall assisted with the lifeboat preparations and was put in charge of lifeboat No 2, being rescued by the *Carpathia*. After the sinking, Boxhall continued to work for White Star Line until his retirement in 1940 and served with the Royal Navy during World War I. He died on 25 April 1967 and his ashes were scattered at 41°46′N 50°14′W, the point he had calculated 55 years earlier as being where the *Titanic* sank.

Harold Bride – The junior wireless operator on board the *Titanic*, Bride (aged 22) was in bed when the ship collided with the iceberg. He joined Phillips who operated the wireless whilst Bride relayed messages to and from Captain Smith. As the power supply failed, Smith told Bride and Phillips that they had done their duty and were relieved from their posts. Bride assisted in efforts to free collapsible lifeboat B from the roof of the officers' quarters. When the lifeboat was washed off, Bride found himself under the capsized lifeboat. He and 15 others were rescued from the lifeboat by the *Carpathia*. He then assisted the *Carpathia*'s wireless operator, Harold Cottam, in sending messages from the survivors. Bride was met in New York by Guglielmo Marconi himself and sold his exclusive story to the *New York Times* for $1,000 before giving evidence

to both the US and British inquiries. He continued to work at sea until the early 1920s and died on 29 April 1956.

Gaspare Gatti – Known as Luigi, Gatti (aged 37) was born in Italy and emigrated to Britain. He ran two restaurants in London – Gatti's Adelphi and Gatti's Strand – and held the concession for the à la carte restaurants on board both the *Olympic* and the *Titanic*, which he staffed with employees – mainly Italian – from his

London establishments. Gatti's body was recovered by the *Minia* and he was buried in Halifax, Nova Scotia, on 10 May 1912. His recovered possessions were returned to his British widow, save for a single dollar bill from his wallet, which was sent to his family in Italy.

Wallace Hartley and the band – The bandleader who famously played on whilst the liner sank, Hartley (aged 33) was employed by C W & F N Black, which supplied musicians to both White Star and Cunard. Despite his reluctance to sail as he'd recently got engaged, he agreed to lead the eight-member band on board the *Titanic*. Following the collision, Hartley and the band played music to help maintain some semblance of calm whilst the lifeboats were loaded. It was reported by many of the survivors that the band carried on playing during the *Titanic*'s final moments. There has always been some debate as to the final music played. Some

◀ Harold Bride.
▼ Wallace Hartley.

survivors claimed it was the popular hymn '*Nearer, my God, to Thee*', but Harold Bride claimed that it was another popular hymn, '*Autumn*' ('*Songe d'Automne*'). Hartley's body was recovered and buried in Colne, Lancashire.

The members of the *Titanic*'s band were pianist W Theodore Brailey (aged 24), bass violinist Fred Clarke (aged 30), violinists John (Jock) Hume (aged 28) and Belgian, Georges Krins (aged 23), and cellists Percy Cornelius Taylor (aged 32), John Wesley Woodward (aged 32) and Frenchman Roger Bricoux (aged 20). Of the seven, only the bodies of Clarke and Hume were recovered by the *Mackay-Bennett* and both were buried in Nova Scotia.

Charles Lightoller – The most senior member of the *Titanic*'s crew to survive, Lightoller (aged 38) was retiring to bed when the collision occurred. He decided to wait until summoned rather than join the panic. He was set to work assisting the allocation of passengers to lifeboats before being thrown into the sea as the ship sank. The force of one of the funnels crashing into the sea pushed him towards collapsible lifeboat B, which had been overturned. Lightoller helped some 30 men to climb aboard the lifeboat. After the sinking, Lightoller worked for White Star Line but, tainted by the disaster, found it difficult to achieve promotion and resigned shortly after. He served with distinction during both World War I and World War II, where he commanded one of the 'little ships' that helped rescue British and Allied soldiers from the beaches of Dunkirk in 1940. He died on 8 December 1952.

Look-outs – It was Frederick Fleet (aged 24), in the crow's nest with Reginald Lee (aged c. 41), who spotted the iceberg and warned the bridge. Having been relieved, Fleet helped to crew lifeboat No 6 which was later picked up by the *Carpathia*. Fleet continued with White Star until August 1912 – the company tended to regard the surviving officers and crew as unfortunate reminders of the tragedy – and then transferred to Union-Castle. He continued at sea until 1936 and then worked at Harland & Wolff. Fleet committed suicide on 10 January 1965 shortly after the death of his wife and having been evicted

◄ Charles Lightoller.

◄◄ Members of the band from the *Titanic*.

by his brother-in-law. Lee escaped the sinking ship on board lifeboat No 13. After testifying to the British Inquiry, he returned to sea but died of pneumonia on 6 August 1913 whilst serving on the *Kenilworth Castle*.

The other look-outs were in their berths when the iceberg struck. Due on duty again at midnight, George Hogg (aged 29) and Alfred Evans (aged 24) dressed and headed for the crow's nest

where they remained for 20 minutes before descending to the boat deck to assist in the loading of the lifeboats. Hogg assisted the crewing of lifeboat No 7. At the British Inquiry Hogg raised the question of the lack of binoculars in the crow's nest. Evans escaped on board lifeboat No 15. He died in 1974.

Archie Jewell (aged 23) was one of the crew members on board lifeboat No 7. After the sinking, Jewell answered some 331 questions at the British Inquiry. He returned to sea after the tragedy and was killed on 17 April 1917

▲ Second class passenger Lawrence Beesley.

when the SS *Donegal* was torpedoed by a German submarine. George Symons (aged 24) was put in charge of lifeboat No 1 – the infamous 'Millionaires' Boat' on which the Duff-Gordon party made their escape.

Harold Lowe – Fifth Officer Lowe (aged 29) was soundly asleep when the iceberg was struck, not waking until around 30 minutes later. Apprised of the situation, he dressed, grabbed his revolver and started to assist in the lowering of the lifeboats. At about 1.30am, Lowe and Sixth Officer Moody agreed that

▲ Harold Lowe.

◄ Look-out point, seen here on the front mast of the *Titanic*.

▶ William
Murdoch.
▶▶ John
Phillips.

each should take charge of one of the surviving lifeboats, with Lowe taking control of No 14. Lowe was forced to fire his revolver three times to prevent passengers endangering the lifeboat in their panic. With lifeboat No 14 safely launched, Lowe gathered together a number of lifeboats and, as the ship sank, determined to return to the scene to rescue those still in the water but was overruled by those already on board who feared that additional survivors would swamp the lifeboats. Eventually, after the majority of the cries from the water had died down, Lowe returned to the scene and plucked a handful of additional survivors from the water. Lowe next turned his attention to collapsible lifeboat A, which was in danger of sinking, and saved those on board. Lowe served with the Royal Naval Reserve during World War I and died on 12 May 1944.

James Moody – Sixth Officer Moody (aged 24) took look-out Fred Fleet's call, asking what he had seen and received the response 'Iceberg, right ahead'. Following the collision, Moody assisted with the launching of lifeboats No 12, 14 and 16 and discussed with Fifth Officer Lowe the need for an officer to be on board each of the lifeboats as it was launched. Moody, allocated to lifeboat No 16, was last spotted trying with others to launch collapsible lifeboat A and died as the ship sank.

William Murdoch – First Officer Murdoch (aged 39) was in command of the *Titanic* when the iceberg was spotted and struck. He gave the commands 'full speed astern' and 'hard a-starboard' to try to avoid the collision. Murdoch was put in charge of evacuation on the starboard side and was last seen trying to release collapsible lifeboat A. His body was never recovered.

John (Jack) Phillips – The senior of the two Marconi-employed wireless operators on board the *Titanic*, Phillips (aged 25) had been trying to catch up with messages that had accumulated from earlier in the day when the wireless had failed and had received a number of warnings about the presence of ice in the area. Following the collision, Phillips was joined by his junior, Harold Bride, and they continued issuing calls for assistance and 'SOS' messages until the power gradually faded and the water rose. On Captain Smith's instruction, they were relieved of their duties. Another crew member

attempted to steal Phillips's life jacket, but Bride spotted this and held the miscreant whilst Phillips knocked the man out. There is some dispute as to the fate of Phillips; according to some

heroes of the night.

Herbert (Bert) Pitman – Third Officer Pitman (aged 34) was off duty at the time of the accident. He was ordered to assist in the preparation of the lifeboats on the starboard side. First Officer Murdoch ordered Pitman to take charge of lifeboat No 5. Pitman moved the lifeboat some 400 yards away from the ship as the *Titanic* sank but, hearing the cries of those in the water, ordered the lifeboat crew back

▲ Captain Edward Smith.

▶ Herbert Pitman.

▶▶ Henry Wilde.

he was on board collapsible lifeboat B but died before the *Carpathia* picked up the survivors but others believe he failed to make it to the lifeboat. As a result of his efforts in trying to maintain contact for as long as possible, Phillips is widely regarded as one of the towards the site. The crew refused, fearing that the lifeboat would get overloaded and Pitman reluctantly rescinded his order. It was a decision that he'd regret for the rest of his life. Pitman and the other survivors on board lifeboat No 5 were rescued by the *Carpathia*. After the sinking, Pitman worked with White Star Line until the early 1920s, when he joined Shaw, Savill & Albion Co Ltd. He finally retired in 1946 and died on 7 December 1961.

Edward Smith – The captain of the *Titanic*, Edward Smith (aged 62) was one of White Star Line's most experienced officers. Smith's fate, other than that he died when the ship sank, is unknown; his body was never recovered.

Henry Wilde – Not initially destined to serve on board the *Titanic*, Wilde (aged 39) had been transferred from the *Olympic* on 3 April as chief officer, replacing Murdoch who became first officer. Wilde was off duty when the iceberg was struck, but was roused and assisted with the loading of the even-numbered lifeboats on the port side. He was seen trying to detach the collapsible lifeboats A and B from the roof of the officers' quarters and did not survive.

Notable Passengers

Thomas Andrews – Co-designer of the White Star Line's new Olympic class liners in conjunction with Harland & Wolff's chairman Lord Pirrie and general manager Alexander Carlisle, Andrews (aged 39) was managing director and head of the shipyard's draughting department when the ships were ordered. Andrews was one of the party of Harland & Wolff personnel on board, as was usual on each vessel's maiden voyage. After the collision Andrews assessed the damage with Captain Smith and, having seen the mail bags from the post room floating 24 feet above the keel, realised both that the vessel was doomed and that the number of lifeboats was inadequate. During the ship's last hours he spent the time rousing passengers and getting them to put on life jackets and head for the lifeboat stations. Andrews was last spotted standing in the first class smoking room in front of a painting showing the entrance to Plymouth Sound. He is presumed to have perished as the ship sank.

John Jacob Astor IV – Coming from one of the wealthiest families in the USA, Astor (aged 47) was returning to New York with his pregnant 18-year-old wife. The Astor family had interests in the fur trade, real estate, hotels and much more, but Astor himself was more than a simple businessman. He had served in the army during the Spanish-American War, written a science-fiction novel and was also an inventor with several patented inventions. On the *Titanic*, the Astor party included a valet, maid and nurse and the couple's pet dog, an Airedale terrier named Kitty. Once the ship struck the iceberg, Astor ensured that his wife was allocated a place on board a lifeboat and, mentioning that his wife was pregnant, sought to board as well. When told that it was women and children first, he stood back. Astor seems to have been crushed when the first funnel collapsed. His body, covered in soot, was recovered on 22 April and was one of the first to be claimed. He was buried in New York.

Lawrence Beesley – This English schoolmaster rose to prominence as a result of his book, *The Loss of the*

SS Titanic: Its Story and its Lessons by One of the Survivors, published in June 1912. Beesley (aged 34) was a second class passenger, and commented on the collision with the iceberg as 'a more than usual dancing of the mattress on which I sat. Nothing more than that – no sound of a crash or of anything else; no sense of

▲ John Jacob Astor.

◄ Thomas Andrews.

▲ Lawrence Beesley using the ship's gym with a lady friend.

▶ Sample of the first class passenger list.

Replying in the negative, Beesley was told to get on board. He died aged 89 on 14 April 1967 – exactly 55 years after the ship sank.

Karl Behr – A US lawyer, Behr (aged 26) was perhaps better known as a tennis player, having played in the Men's Doubles at Wimbledon and for the USA in the Davis Cup. He was aboard the *Titanic* in pursuit of his courtship of Helen Monypeny Newsom, whose mother disapproved of the romance and had taken her daughter to Europe to escape Behr's attentions. Manufacturing an excuse for a business trip to Europe, Behr booked himself on the *Titanic* from Cherbourg in order to continue the relationship. On the night of the sinking Behr, Miss Newsom and others went to the starboard boat deck and one of the party enquired whether all could board lifeboat No 5. White Star Line managing director J Bruce Ismay, who was assisting, concurred and the entire party boarded. Behr was one of a committee of survivors to honour the bravery of Captain Rostron and the crew of the *Carpathia* with an engraved silver cup for the captain and medals to each of the 320 crew members. Behr and Miss Newsom were married the following

shock, no jar that felt like one heavy body meeting another.' He escaped on lifeboat No 13 when, as the boat was being launched, he was asked by the crew member in charge if there were any women and children around.

year. Behr later went into banking before his death on 15 October 1949.

Millvina Dean – At just nine weeks old, Millvina Dean was not only the youngest survivor of the sinking of the *Titanic*, but also the last remaining survivor, passing away on 31 May 2009 at the age of 97. The Deans were emigrating to Wichita, Kansas, where Millvina's father had family and hoped to open a tobacconist's shop. Owing to a coal strike, the Deans had been transferred from another White Star liner to the *Titanic*, travelling as third class passengers. Millvina's father felt the ship's collision with the iceberg and, after investigating, returned to his cabin telling his wife to dress the children and go up on deck. Millvina escaped with her mother and brother in lifeboat No 10, but her father was lost with the ship. The family returned to England but it was not until she was eight years old that Millvina learned about the tragedy from her mother. In 2008, at the age of 96, Dean was forced to sell several family possessions with *Titanic* associations to pay for her private medical care following a broken hip, and in February 2009 she announced that she would be selling more items.

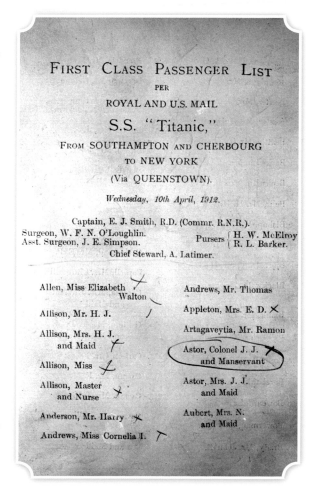

The Millvina Fund was set up in April 2009 by the Belfast, British and International Titanic Societies with the exclusive aim of taking care of Millvina Dean's nursing home bills. Irish author and campaigning journalist Don Mullan challenged the director and stars of the film *Titanic* to match his donation to the fund. Actors Leonardo DiCaprio and Kate Winslet jointly contributed $20,000 and singer Celine Dion and director James Cameron each donated $10,000 to the fund. Millvina Dean died from pneumonia on the 98th anniversary of the launching of the *Titanic*.

Sir Cosmo Duff-Gordon – The fifth Baronet of Halkin (aged 49), whose family had owned a sherry bodega in Spain since 1772 and whose family name was carried by a well-known brand of gin, was a prominent sportsman – representing Great Britain in fencing, for example – and landowner. Sir Cosmo and his wife were to become infamous survivors of the *Titanic* by escaping in a lifeboat designed for 40 with only three friends and seven crew members on board. The subsequent inquiries exonerated them from any criticism as, although Duff-Gordon was aware of the tradition of women and children first, he contended – and was supported in this by other survivors – that none were present when the boat was launched. The lifeboat's passengers were safely rescued by the *Carpathia*. Duff-Gordon's reputation was besmirched by the fact that he had offered each of the seven crew members £5 to replace their lost kit. This had been prompted by the complaints of one of the seven crew that they had lost everything in the sinking, but appeared to others more like a bribe, particularly as Duff-Gordon's agent offered further inducements to the seven prior to the two inquiries. Duff-Gordon died on 20 April 1931.

Dorothy Gibson – A noted American model and actress in the silent film industry and on stage, Dorothy Gibson (aged 22) was returning from Italy where she had been on holiday with her mother. On the night of the collision, the two women had been playing bridge with others in the lounge. When the boat struck the iceberg, they made their way to the boat deck and managed to escape on lifeboat No 7, the first to be launched. Arriving back home, Gibson was encouraged by

her manager to write and to star in a film about the sinking. *Saved from the Titanic* was released in 1912 and in the film she wore the same clothing – a white silk evening dress with cardigan and polo coat – that she'd worn during her escape. Dorothy Gibson retired from filmmaking shortly after *Saved from the Titanic*. Following a divorce, she married Jules Brulatour in 1917, one of the founders of Universal Studios, but the marriage was annulled two years later. She spent the rest of her life in France apart from a four-year period in Italy during World War II, where she was imprisoned for a time before escaping. She died on 17 February 1946.

▲ Sir Cosmo Duff-Gordon with members of the British Fencing team.

▲ Benjamin Guggenheim.

▶ J Bruce Ismay.

Archibald Gracie – An American military historian returning home to Washington DC having been researching the 1812 war between Britain and the USA, Colonel Gracie (aged 53) had boarded the *Titanic* at Southampton. On the evening of the sinking, he had retired to bed and was awoken by a jolt. Dressing, he ascended to the boat deck where he assisted the female friends he had been chaperoning into lifeboats. Following the launch of the last lifeboat, Gracie helped Second Officer Lightoller and others to free the four collapsible lifeboats. As the ship started to sink, Gracie was drawn down by the undertow but managed to free himself and swim to the surface. Along with a couple of dozen others, he was able to

get on board collapsible lifeboat B. As dawn approached, Lightoller used his whistle to attract the other lifeboats and Gracie transferred to No 12, later to be rescued by the *Carpathia*. After returning to New York, Gracie researched the sinking with a view to publication, but his health had suffered as a result of prolonged exposure to the cold water and he died on 4 December 1912. His book, *The Truth about the Titanic*, was published in 1913.

Benjamin Guggenheim – An American businessman and the fifth son of the mining magnate Meyer Guggenheim, Benjamin Guggenheim (aged 46) was estranged from his wife and boarded the *Titanic* at Cherbourg on 10 April with his mistress, the French singer Léontine Aubart, her maid and his valet and chauffeur. When awakened, both Guggenheim and his valet were initially reluctant to believe that the ship had struck an iceberg but got the women on board lifeboat No 9. Although Guggenheim reassured the maid in German, 'It's just a repair. Tomorrow the *Titanic* will go on again', he was aware of the true position. Guggenheim and his valet changed into evening wear and he was heard to comment, 'We've dressed up in our best and are prepared to go down like gentlemen.' Guggenheim, his valet and chauffeur perished as the ship sank, with their bodies never being recovered. Both women survived, dying within months of each other 52 years later.

J Bruce Ismay – By the time of the *Titanic*'s maiden voyage, Ismay (aged 49) had risen to become the managing director of White Star Line, the shipping company founded by his father, Thomas Ismay. He decided to sail on *Titanic*'s maiden voyage and, following the ship's collision, survived as one of the passengers on board collapsible lifeboat C before being transferred to the *Carpathia*. Ismay was roundly criticised in both Britain and the United States for his survival when women and children had perished, although the evidence suggests that he was active in encouraging as many as possible on board the lifeboats before being encouraged to board when he was assured there were no female passengers in the vicinity. He testified to both the British and US inquiries and resigned as president of International Mercantile Marine in 1913, but remained active in shipping circles thereafter. He died on 15 October 1937.

Francis (Frank) Millet – An American painter and writer, Millet (aged 65) had joined the ship at Cherbourg after accompanying a friend and fellow passenger on a sojourn to Europe. He posted a letter from Queenstown in which he wrote, 'Queer lot of people on the ship. There

▲
William T Stead.
▶ Isidor Straus.

around like pet lambs.' Millet was one of the party that played cards and drank in the first class smoking room. He did not survive the sinking but his body was ultimately recovered by the *Mackay-Bennett* and buried in Massachusetts.

William T Stead – A noted British journalist and campaigner, Stead (aged 62) had been invited by President Taft to address a peace congress due to be held in New York on 21 April. Earlier in his career, in an article in the *Pall Mall Gazette* of 22 March 1886, Stead had warned of the dangers of major loss of life following a mid-Atlantic collision if the vessels concerned lacked sufficient lifeboats. Six years later, in the 1892 Christmas edition of *Review of Reviews*, he wrote a fictional account of a transatlantic liner sinking after a collision with an iceberg. Following the collision, Stead assisted a number of women and children into lifeboats. He was last spotted sitting in the first class smoking room, reading a book. He died as the ship sank.

Isidor Straus – A German by birth, Isidor Straus (aged 67) – also known as Isadore Strauss – had become a prominent businessman based in the USA. He was co-owner of Macy's, the

are a number of obnoxious, ostentatious American women, the scourge of any place they infest and worse on shipboard than anywhere.' Mentioning the number of passengers that had brought pets with them, he said, 'Many of them carry tiny dogs, and lead husbands famous department store, and served briefly as a member of Congress. He was travelling with his wife Ida, who was offered a berth on a lifeboat. She refused, telling her husband, 'We have been together for many years. Where you go, I go.' Although offered a place on the grounds of his age following pressure from Colonel Gracie, Straus declined. The couple's maid boarded the lifeboat but Ida refused. Straus's body was recovered and buried in New York; that of his wife was never found.

John B Thayer – Vice-president of the Pennsylvania Railroad, Thayer (aged 49), with his wife Marian and son John (Jack), boarded at Cherbourg after spending time with the American consul general in Berlin. After attending a party hosted by prominent American businessman George Widener, they had retired and were preparing for bed when the collision occurred. Jack, with an overcoat over his pyjamas, went on deck to investigate. He returned and changed into a tweed suit with several vests in order to keep warm, and then all three went on deck. Marian Thayer escaped on lifeboat No 4, but John B Thayer remained on board to await his fate and his body was never discovered. Jack Thayer (aged 17) was not allocated a lifeboat berth and got separated from his parents. As the ship sank, being a strong swimmer, he leapt overboard to try to swim for safety and eventually reached the upturned collapsible B to join a number of other survivors on board. He was rescued with the others by lifeboats No 4 and 12. Ironically, whilst his mother was on lifeboat No 4, Jack was allocated to No 12 as neither was in a condition to recognise the other. They were rescued by the *Carpathia* and returned home to Haverford, Pennsylvania. The death of one of his two sons during World War II, combined with depression, caused Jack Thayer to commit suicide on 20 September 1945.

Other Major Figures

Harold Cottam – The wireless operator on board the *Carpathia*, Cottam (aged 21) was a direct employee of the Marconi Company rather than of Cunard. The *Carpathia*'s radio equipment had a range of 250 miles and he was the only qualified radio operator on board. He had been on the point of retiring to bed, having been on duty since the early morning, but was waiting for a response from another ship when he heard the *Titanic*'s distress signal. After informing Captain Rostron of the collision, he remained in contact with the *Titanic* until the latter ceased transmissions. After the *Carpathia* had picked up survivors, Cottam was assisted in relaying messages to and from shore by the surviving *Titanic* wireless operator, Harold Bride. Cottam continued to work as a wireless operator until his retirement. He died on 30 May 1984.

Stanley Lord – The captain of the Leyland Line ship SS *Californian*, Lord (aged 35) was one of the more controversial figures in the *Titanic* story,

as the *Californian* was sufficiently close to the site of the tragedy to see the rockets being fired from the stricken ship. It was estimated that the two ships were less than 20 miles apart – the subsequent US and British inquiries

▼ RMS *Carpathia*.

suggested that the two ships were even closer – and members of the crew on board the *Titanic* were aware of the lights of another ship in the distance. It was not until the morning of 15 April that Lord received a message from the *Frankfurt* that the *Titanic* had sunk and the *Californian* reached the site of the sinking at 8.30am. Lord was interviewed by the US Inquiry on 26 April and, once back in Britain, he was also interviewed by the British Inquiry. The latter concluded that, had the *Californian* responded to the distress signals, the ship '… might have saved many if not all of the lives that were lost.' Although never convicted of any crime, Lord's name was undoubtedly sullied by the criticism and he spent much of the remainder of his life trying to restore his reputation. He left the employment of Leyland Line in August 1912, although whether he resigned or was dismissed is unclear, and joined the Nitrate Producers Steamship Co the following year. He remained with the company until he resigned on health grounds in July 1928. Lord died on 24 January 1962. In 1992, the British Marine Accident Investigation Branch undertook a review of the evidence. Although unable to answer many of the questions surrounding the actions of the *Californian* that night, the report concluded that the *Californian* did not see the *Titanic* but did see the rockets and that the distance between the two ships was much greater than was originally believed in the 1912 inquiry. However, the report agreed that since the *Californian* had seen the rockets, Lord should have acted.

Arthur Rostron – The captain of the *Carpathia*, Rostron's professionalism was a significant factor in the rescue of the *Titanic's* survivors. Following receipt of the distress signals from the *Titanic*, Rostron (aged 42) made for the stricken ship as quickly as he could, exceeding the *Carpathia's* maximum speed of 14 knots by achieving 17 knots. Even so, the ship took three and a half hours to reach the site of the sinking and arrived in the early hours of the morning. Under Rostron's command, the *Carpathia* picked up more than 700 survivors before heading back to New York. Rostron gave evidence to both the US and British inquiries and was presented with a silver cup by grateful survivors. Rostron continued his career with Cunard, becoming a Commander of

◀ Arthur Rostron.

◀◀ Stanley Lord.

the Order of the British Empire in 1919 and receiving his knighthood seven years later. In July 1928 Rostron became Commodore of the Cunard Line before retirement in 1931. He died on 4 November 1940.

The Maiden Voyage

▶ The *Titanic* departs from Southampton dock.

Following the arrival of the *Titanic* at Southampton and the loading of the stores, the ship was scheduled to start her maiden voyage on Wednesday 10 April 1912. The crew started to arrive from 5.18am onwards and Captain Smith boarded at about 7.30am, heading straight for his cabin to be briefed by Chief Officer Wilde.

Later in the morning the passengers started to arrive. The third class passengers, who boarded through the aft entrances on C deck, embarked between 9.30am and 11.00am. Following embarkation, the third class passengers underwent a medical examination to ensure they appeared healthy, as the US immigration officials could refuse entry to those deemed medically unfit. The medical inspection was particularly rigorous for non-British citizens, many of whom were Scandinavian.

At 11.30am the Boat Train from London Waterloo arrived with the more select first and second class passengers.

The first class passengers entered by way of gangways amidships to deck B and were provided with guidebooks to the ship to enable them to get the most from their crossing. Stewards assisted both first and second class passengers to their cabins.

By the end of embarkation some 900 passengers had boarded the *Titanic*. By noon the great ship was ready to make her departure from Southampton. A small number of crew members, who had been allowed additional time on shore (and who had visited local pubs as a result), failed to make it back to the ship in time. A number of replacement

Five tugs gently eased the *Titanic* away from the dockside. As the massive liner gradually emerged from her dock and clear of the harbour wall, the swell caused by her passage caused the SS *New York* to break her moorings and to start to drift dangerously close to the *Titanic*. The situation was rescued by prompt action on the part of Captain Gale on board the tug *Vulcan*, who at the second attempt managed to get a line aboard the *New York* and manoeuvre her away from danger. The two ships were no further than four feet apart when Gale's action saved the day, and the incident delayed the *Titanic* by about an hour.

The liner now set course for Cherbourg, dropping anchor there at 6.30pm, still an hour behind schedule. An additional 142 first class, 30 second and 102 third class passengers were waiting to board, whilst 15 first class and seven second class passengers waited to disembark. These cross-channel passengers had been charged £1 10s and £1 each respectively for their brief trip from Southampton. Two tenders – one for third class passengers and the other for first and second class travellers – ferried passengers out from the harbour to the liner.

◄ Tugged out of Southampton, the *Titanic* would soon be on her way to Cherbourg.

crew members, held on stand-by, took the place of those who had failed to arrive on time.

At 12 noon, with the Trinity House pilot on board, the Blue Peter – the flag that indicated imminent departure – was raised on the foremast and three sharp blasts were given on the ship's whistle.

LITTLE BOOK OF **TITANIC**

Once the passengers were aboard, the *Titanic* set course for its next port of call, Queenstown in County Cork, Ireland, at about 8.00pm. The ship reached Queenstown on the morning of 11 April. Shortly before reaching port, Captain Smith ordered an emergency drill. This tested the emergency doors and other safety equipment, although there is no record to indicate whether the lifeboats, two of which had been tested at Southampton, were tested.

As at Cherbourg, passengers were ferried to the ship by two tenders, but there was a further slight delay. As well as 120 first class, seven second class and 113 third class passengers, 1,385 bags of mail were ferried out to the ship. Seven passengers and one crew member also disembarked at Queenstown. Amongst these was Francis Browne, a pioneering and obsessive photographer, who had taken pictures of the near miss with the *New York* at Southampton as well as portraits of a number of the prominent people on board, including Captain Smith. At 1.30pm the *Titanic* weighed anchor and headed towards the Atlantic. One of the steerage passengers had brought his bagpipes on board and as Ireland slipped astern he played the tune '*Erin's Lament*'.

Whilst the *Titanic* was at Queenstown, J Bruce Ismay – as he later admitted to the US Inquiry – had a private conversation with the ship's chief engineer, Joseph Bell. According to Ismay's testimony, 'It was our intention, if we had fine weather on Monday afternoon or Tuesday, to drive the ship at full speed… The *Titanic*, being a new ship, we were gradually working her up.' However, Ismay also admitted that he hadn't discussed the possibility of a high-speed run with Captain Smith.

Transatlantic steamships followed set 'tracks' when passing to and fro from northern Europe to the United States. Usually the southern track, used from January 15 to August 23, was comparatively free from ice. However, the winter of 1911/12 had proved to be milder than most, with the result that the Arctic ice sheet was breaking up more rapidly than usual and icebergs had been drifting south into the shipping lanes. Captain Smith would have been aware of the presence of ice as the trade press had been reporting it in the months preceding *Titanic's* maiden voyage.

◀ The *Titanic* departs Queenstown, New York bound.

During the ship's first 24 hours at sea – from noon on Thursday 11 April through to noon on Friday 12 April – everything seemed to be progressing well and some 386 nautical miles were covered. In the wireless room Jack Phillips and Harold Bride were busy taking and receiving messages on behalf of passengers, whilst also receiving messages from other ships regarding navigational conditions. By lunchtime on 12 April, the *Titanic* had received five messages from other ships ahead of her, warning of ice. These were followed by a further four later in the day. The ice was, however, still far ahead of the ship and so the ship made

more rapid progress on the succeeding two days as the new engines were gradually put through their paces – achieving 519 nautical miles by noon on 13 April and a further 546 nautical miles by noon on Sunday 14 April.

On the morning of 14 April, which had dawned cold and clear but with a slight haze, the first of the day's sequence of ice warnings was received, when at 9.00am the captain of the *Caronia* sent the *Titanic* a message saying westbound steamers were encountering ice. Under White Star regulations, a lifeboat drill should have been held that morning, but these were not popular with the crew and, in light of the cold weather, it was decided not to hold the practice. As it was a Sunday, a religious service was held.

At 1.42pm a further warning of ice was received from the *Baltic*. It would appear that Captain Smith passed the warning on to J Bruce Ismay in order to alert him to the presence of ice and that, inexplicably, Ismay held on to the message until the early evening. During the course of the afternoon further warnings of ice were received, but the ship did not change direction until 5.50pm, when a planned change of course took place.

At 7.30pm Second Officer Lightoller took an accurate reading of the ship's position using his sextant, which he passed to Fourth Officer Boxhall for calculation. Contrary to standing orders, Captain Smith was not on the bridge at this time, but was attending the Wideners' private party in the à la carte restaurant. During the course of the evening, Lightoller had been noting a steady drop in the outside temperature; by the time that Smith returned to the bridge at 9.00pm, the outside temperature had dropped to 33°F (1°C), but the sea was calm and the stars were clear in the moonless sky. Lightoller had already noted in the night order book the necessity of keeping a sharp look out for icebergs. Based on the warnings he had seen, Lightoller's calculations suggested that ice would be encountered from about 11.30pm, although other bridge officers had calculated a slightly earlier time. Captain Smith and Lightoller had a conversation about the weather and the visibility of icebergs in such climatic conditions.

The captain retired to his cabin at about 9.20pm, having issued instructions to Lightoller that he was to be roused immediately if anything untoward occurred. The wireless operators were engaged in handing transmissions to and from passengers – the business from which Marconi derived its income – so a message received at 9.40pm warning of ice in the area the *Titanic* was approaching was not passed directly to the bridge.

At 10.30pm the *Titanic* passed the *Rappahannock* with the latter signalling by Morse lamp a further warning of the presence of ice. Although the message was acknowledged, there was no reduction in the ship's speed, which

◀ Binoculars retrieved from the *Titanic*

▼ A telephone from the *Titanic*, perhaps used by Fleet calling the bridge.

rudder would have impaired her manoeuvrability.

Fifty feet up in the crow's nest, the look-outs had been keeping a wary eye out for ice and at around 11.00pm they noted that the previously clear night had developed a slight haze. White Star Line was unusual at the time in that it only employed look-outs who had gone to the expense of having an eye test. They were also, in theory, provided with a pair of binoculars, which were notionally in the charge of the Second Officer but which were stored in a specially-built cupboard in the crow's nest itself. When the original Second Officer, David Blair, was replaced, he took with him the key to the cupboard in the crow's nest but left his binoculars. During the crossing from Southampton to Cherbourg the look-outs had reported the fact that no binoculars had been issued to them, although they had had them during the trip from Belfast to Southampton.

At 11.39pm, look-out Fred Fleet grabbed the ship's bell and gave it three pulls in order to alert the bridge of an obstruction ahead. According to the statement he made later to the British Inquiry, Fleet had spotted 'A black object, high above the water, dead

was still around 22 knots, or in the course that the ship was taking. It was unfortunate that the *Rappahannock* was not fitted with a wireless as, apart from the mystery ship, she was probably the closest vessel to the *Titanic* when the iceberg was struck, although a damaged

ahead.' He then called the bridge using the telephone and told Sixth Officer Moody that he had seen an 'Iceberg right ahead'. This was acknowledged and Fleet noticed an almost immediate turn to port.

First Officer Murdoch, standing on the open wing of the bridge, saw the iceberg on the starboard side at a distance of some 800 yards. Returning to the bridge, he ordered the ship to turn 'hard a-starboard' whilst also using the engine room telegraph to instruct the engineers to 'Stop: full speed

astern'. (On the *Titanic*'s sea trial, the emergency stop had required 850 yards even when travelling at a lower speed than that on the evening of 14 April; it was inevitable that the ship would strike an object some 800 yards away – the big question was how severely.)

Some 39 seconds after Fleet's conversation with Moody, the ship struck the iceberg. There was contact for about 10 seconds as the berg scraped along the starboard side of the ship, creating a gash some 300 feet in length around 15 feet above the keel.

▲ Latitude 41°46´N and longitude 50°14´W, the place where the *Titanic* sank.

◀ Captain Smith had retired to his cabin prior to the disaster.

The Final Moments

Between the collision with the iceberg at 11.40pm and the *Titanic* actually sinking at 2.20am, there was more than two and a half hours of activity, some of it frenetic and some less so. Many of those on board showed considerable courage, whilst the behaviour of others was perhaps less commendable.

Most passengers were unaware of the collision and those who did feel the impact commented on how slight it felt. Passenger Jack Thayer commented, 'If I had a brimful glass of water in my hand, not a drop would have been spilled.' Mrs Astor initially thought that it was some mishap in the kitchen, whilst J Bruce Ismay was awakened by what he thought was the loss of a propeller. One of the passengers in the first class smoking room, Hugh Woolner, noted '…a sort of stopping, a sort – not exactly shock, but a sort of slowing down. And then we felt a rip that gave a sort of slight twist to the whole room. Everybody, so far as I could see, stood up and a number

of men walked out rapidly through the swinging doors on the port side and ran along to the rail that was behind the mast.' The journalist William Stead was on deck when the collision happened and both he and his companion, Father Thomas Byles, thought that little of note had happened.

The reality, however, was that below the waterline the huge gash had been scored about 15 feet above the keel. It has subsequently been estimated that the total area exposed to water flooding in was no more than 12 square feet, but this extended over a considerable distance, with the result that sea water started to enter the forepeak tank (the forwardmost division of the hull, often used in ships as a ballast tank), holds 1, 2 and 3, and the forward boiler room (No 6). The ship could remain afloat provided that only two of the watertight compartments were flooded, but the collision damage caused the bow section to lower in the water and the water level to rise above the bulkheads

◄ An illustration depicting the damage caused by the iceberg.

separating the watertight compartments. Only the first of the bulkheads (nearest the bow) extended up to deck C; bulkheads two and 11-15 extended to deck D, but those from three to 10 extended only to deck E. With the water reaching boiler room No 6 and the bow section settling deeper in the water, the level of water on board was rising above deck E.

Following the collision, Captain Smith returned to the bridge and Murdoch briefed him on what had occurred, 'We have struck an iceberg. I put her hard a-starboard and run the engines full astern, but it was too close; she hit it. I intended to port around it, but she hit before I could do any more.' Murdoch then said, 'The watertight doors are closed, sir.' Apart from the automatic doors on the lower decks, there were also a number of watertight doors that could be closed manually. These non-automatic doors, hinged and secured by use of 12 clips, were closed but they would have been of little practical use once the water started to rise above the level of the bulkheads.

The ship's predicament was outlined to Captain Smith by Thomas Andrews, when the two of them made a 10-minute inspection of the damage. Andrews was acutely aware that water entering into more than two of the ship's watertight compartments meant that the vessel was effectively doomed. By 12.30am, some 16,000 tons of water had already entered the ship and, with the level already rising above deck E, the *Titanic* was destined to sink.

As the duty officers arrived on the bridge, they were given tasks; curiously, the off-duty officers (such as Lowe who was awakened by the commotion outside his cabin on the boat deck at 12.45am) weren't roused to assist in organising the passengers and crew. Boxhall was sent down below to inspect the damage; he reported back 15 minutes later that he had found no damage above deck F, but that a postal clerk had informed him of water entering at deck G level.

On his return, shortly after midnight, Boxhall was instructed to calculate the ship's position, which he did using the position calculated by Lightoller from the stars at 7.30pm. This was the notorious 41°46′N/50°14′W, some 13 miles from the ship's actual location at 41°43′N/49°56′W. The inaccuracy could have been caused by a number of

◀ An artist's impression of Captain Smith issuing his 'Last Orders'.

THE FINAL MOMENTS

► Lowering the
first lifeboats.

factors and is probably explicable under the circumstances in which Boxhall was operating. Factors leading to the error may include overestimating the ship's speed by half a knot (22 knots as opposed to the actual speed of 21.5 knots), the subtle changes required to the ship's clock during the period from 7.30pm onwards and the one-knot southerly current through which the *Titanic* was passing. Whatever the cause, the erroneous information was soon being transmitted by Jack Phillips and Harold Bride from the wireless room as they started to issue 'CQD' messages (the distress code used by Marconi operators) at around 12.15am. 'SOS' had been introduced only in 1907, following the International Conference on Wireless Communication at Sea held in Berlin in 1906, and was not yet in universal use. In a subsequent article in the *New York Times*, Bride reported a conversation in the wireless room when he suggested, 'Send SOS; it's the new call, and it may be your last chance to send it.' The *Titanic* later sent out a mixture of CQD and SOS signals.

Amongst the ships in the area was the RMS *Carpathia*. On board, the ship's wireless operator, Harold Cottam, was waiting for a reply to a message that he'd sent earlier to the *Parisian*. Cottam had been on duty since 7.00am and was eager for bed. Whilst waiting for the *Parisian* to respond, he listened in on other transmissions from Cape Cod; becoming aware that the shore station had a number of signals for the *Titanic*, Cottam finally made contact with the White Star liner, asking whether the *Titanic*'s radio operator was aware there was a batch of messages coming through from Cape Cod for him. Phillips responded immediately with 'Come at once. This is a CQD OM [Old Man]' and radioed *Titanic*'s position. Cottam acted immediately; he and the *Carpathia*'s officer of the watch, H V Dean, roused the captain and alerted him to the situation. Captain Rostron responded to the unfolding tragedy with alacrity and, in a masterful display of seamanship, set course for the *Titanic*'s reported position. He was undoubtedly one of the heroes of the night.

Shortly before midnight, J Bruce Ismay came up to the bridge – his first visit there since the voyage began – and was told that the ship was badly damaged and was taking in water at the forepeak and in four of the watertight

compartments. Soon after midnight, Smith ordered Chief Officer Wilde to uncover the lifeboats and First Officer Murdoch began to muster the passengers. Wilde was assisted in his task by look-out George Symons. Second Officer Lightoller was then given permission by the captain to swing the boats out and, at 12.25am, the order was given to start loading them – women and children first.

Below decks, the situation was fast deteriorating. In boiler room No 5 the crew had managed to get the pumps working and were winning the battle to keep the water level down. However, the pressure in the boilers was rising rapidly, causing the safety valves to blow off, and there was a danger that the steam pipes might burst. Just as the order was given to draw the fire, the damaged bulkhead between boiler rooms No 5 and No 6 collapsed, with water rushing in.

Wallace Hartley and his orchestra started playing ragtime numbers in the first class lounge before moving to the boat deck by the port-side entrance to the grand staircase. By this time the water had reached 40 feet above the keel at the forward end of deck E.

Lightoller initially intended to load the lifeboats from A deck and, having ordered the women and children to that level, lowered lifeboat No 4 at about 12.45am. However, the windows on the forward section of A deck were locked and, rather than return the boat to the boat deck and load it from there, Lightoller elected to try to find the key.

Shortly after the order to uncover the lifeboats, Boxhall was instructed to start firing the ship's distress rockets. Manufactured by the Cotton Powder Co Ltd, the rockets – 'socket signals' – were designed to reach a height of 800 feet. A total of 24 of these rockets were brought to the bridge, with the first being launched at around 12.45am. Commenting on the firing of the first rocket Lawrence Beesley said, 'Up it went, higher and higher, with a sea of faces upturned to watch it, and then an explosion that seemed to split the silent night in two.'

The first lifeboat to be launched was No 7 with only 28 people on board. These included the actress Dorothy Gibson, the French aviator Pierre Maréchal, the Pennsylvanian banker James R McGough and stockbroker William T Sloper. Lifeboat No 3 was also being made ready. Aware that the situation might get out of hand, Lowe returned to his cabin to arm himself before heading back to the boat deck to assist with the loading of the lifeboats.

Given that the Sunday morning lifeboat drill had been cancelled and the only testing of the lifeboats had been the brief trial undertaken at Southampton, it is perhaps of little surprise that the launching of the lifeboats proved problematic. Although the instruction had gone out for women and children to be put in the lifeboats, a certain number of male passengers had boarded the early lifeboats; male crew members, however, were supposed to have been on board as they were required to row the lifeboats away from the sinking ship and to maintain order on board them.

Lifeboat No 5 was only partially filled with some 30 women and children, but as no more were nearby Third Officer Pitman, in charge of the boat allowed four male passengers to board. A total of 39 were on board when No 5 was lowered to the water. As it was being lowered, two further male passengers leapt on board, one of them injuring Mrs Annie May Stengel, a first class passenger, as he landed on her.

The chaotic launchings meant that not only were many of the scarce lifeboats lowered with many fewer than the permitted number of passengers on board, but a number also lacked the requisite crew members to handle the boats correctly once in the water. Such was the case with lifeboat No 6; this was launched at 1.00am with only two crew members on board along with 24 women passengers and a male stowaway. As no additional crew members could be allocated, Second Officer Lightoller permitted a male passenger, Major Arthur Peuchen (who claimed to have some knowledge of yachting), to board, however, much of the rowing of the boat was undertaken ultimately by the women passengers led by the indomitable Mrs Molly Brown.

Only about 14 women and children could be found for lifeboat No 3, resulting in 12 male passengers as well as up to 14 crew members being allowed to board. Also on board was a Pekinese dog belonging to first class passenger Henry Sleeper Harper.

Of the lifeboats fitted to the *Titanic*, two – Nos 1 and 2 – were considered emergency boats and were always kept in a state of heightened readiness.

They were, however, smaller (25 feet rather than 30 feet) and had a smaller capacity (40 as opposed to 65) than the other lifeboats. It was lifeboat No 1 that Sir Cosmo Duff-Gordon and his party boarded.

Also being prepared was lifeboat No 8, the boarding of which was again being supervised by Lightoller. Mrs Ida Straus was initially placed on this boat, but as Lightoller refused to allow her husband Isidor to join her, she disembarked, although her maid remained. A group of some 30 third class passengers, women and children, were brought up but few were permitted to board – allocation of berths seems to have been class based with many of the steerage passengers effectively being abandoned to their fate. Lifeboat No 8 was eventually launched with 24 passengers and four members of crew.

Lifeboat No 9 was better filled, with a total of 56 on board – including at least 15 members of crew and nine male passengers. Meanwhile, the ship was developing a more pronounced list to port and a number of passengers were sent to the starboard side in an effort to reduce this. Lifeboat No 10 was lowered with four crew and 51 passengers, including two stowaways – a Japanese and an Armenian. As the boat was lowered, a 56th passenger – described as a 'crazed Italian' – leapt aboard. This was followed by No 11 with some 70 in total – the first boat to be launched with more than the maximum number of persons on board.

Lifeboat No 12 was the next to embark with 40 women and children from second and steerage classes on board plus two crewmen and one first class passenger. By this stage discipline was starting to slip and, before the boat was lowered, Lightoller and a crewman on board had to prevent other passengers attempting to rush the boat.

By the time Officers Lowe and Wilde moved on to launch lifeboat No 14, the situation had deteriorated further and passengers again tried to board without permission. According to one of the crew members, Lowe threatened to shoot any passengers who caused trouble. A teenage boy on board the lifeboat was ordered by Lowe to return to the stricken ship. With 64 on board, including himself, Lowe ordered the boat to be lowered, firing three shots to deter any last minute

◄ An artist's impression of Captain Smith refusing help from men on an upturned lifeboat, when offered the chance of rescue.

THE FINAL MOMENTS

▶ Survivors in a
crowded lifeboat.

attempts to leap on board. As the boat was lowered, the mechanism seized up with the boat some five feet above the water. Lowe reacted by pulling the lever on the Murray's Patented Release Gear, which released both ends of the lifeboat simultaneously. The boat fell into the water with some force, causing it to spring a leak. The boat had to be baled out manually with the use of hats until those on board were rescued by the *Carpathia*.

The next lifeboat into the water was No 16 with 56 passengers and crew on board. As it was being lowered Mrs Leather, one of the stewardesses on board, heard the band still playing. Simultaneously, lifeboat No 13 was lowered on the starboard side, accommodating around 24 crew (including some 16 kitchen staff and stewards), one first class passenger and 38 second and third class passengers, a total of about 63. As the boat was being lowered, one of the crewmen noticed Lawrence Beesley and asked if there were any women and children visible. When Beesley indicated that he couldn't see any, the crewmen instructed Beesley to leap aboard, taking the number on board lifeboat No 13 to

around 64. As the lifeboat was lowered, Beesley noticed what he believed to be the last distress rocket fired from the ship. The lifeboat drifted towards the stern and was in danger of being crushed by lifeboat No 15, which was being lowered at that time. Fortunately, shouts from below were heard and the lowering of No 15 was delayed fractionally. The lifeboat was eventually lowered with 14 crew members, one first class passenger and 53 women from third class, making a total of 68 in all.

On the starboard side, attention now switched to collapsible C, which Murdoch had positioned under the davits used for lifeboat No 3. Six crew members, under the command of Quartermaster Rowe, were allocated to the boat. As order continued to deteriorate, Murdoch was forced to fire his pistol into the air to clear the boat of 'Italians and foreigners who had sneaked into it'. Just as third class passengers were discriminated against, so too were non-British or US citizens. The staff of the à la carte restaurant and the Café Parisien, for example, being largely Italian and neither passengers nor crew were effectively barred from making their way to the boat deck and thus perished.

Luigi Gatti's secretary, Paul Mauge, survived, however; attributing this at the British Inquiry to his being dressed like a passenger. Around 39-44 passengers and crew were loaded on board collapsible C, which was designed to hold 47. Amongst those that made good their escape on this boat was J Bruce Ismay. Again, to prevent any last-minute attempts to leap aboard, shots were fired.

Lightoller's attention was now focused on lifeboat No 2. He discovered it was full of 'dagoes' who he ordered off at gunpoint. He ordered three crew members and Fourth Officer Boxhall to board and 21 passengers were then allowed on, making a total of 25 – again well below the boat's actual capacity of 40. With No 2 launched, Lightoller returned to lifeboat No 4, which had earlier been held up as a result of the locked windows on deck A. After some confusion, with the intended passengers being switched from deck to deck, the windows on deck A had been opened. However, with the ship's increasing list to port, there was now a considerable distance between the deck and the lifeboat. Boat hooks were used to bring the boat closer to the deck and the boat was lashed to the side of the liner. A makeshift ladder allowed the passengers and crew to board.

Amongst the passengers waiting patiently to board lifeboat No 4 were the Astor, Thayer, Widener and Ryerson families. Initially, Lightoller refused permission for 13-year-old Jack Ryerson to board the boat with his mother, but was overruled by the rest of the group. Although the boat with around 40 on board was not full, the men were prevented from entering, in spite of requests from Astor to be allowed to join his pregnant wife. Lifeboat No 4 was lowered at 1.55am with Astor and the other men waving farewell to their wives and reassuring them that they would be on another boat. One of the crewmen on board, greaser Thomas Ranger, heard the band still playing as the lifeboat was lowered.

Whilst there was feverish activity on the boat deck, in the wireless room the two Marconi operators, Jack Phillips and Harold Bride, were hard at work sending out distress messages. As the ship's generator, powered by the boilers, gradually failed so the signals issued by the *Titanic* got gradually fainter and fainter. Shortly after 2.00am, Captain Smith came to the wireless room and relieved Phillips and Bride of their duties; they had done as much as they could and, with the ship's power failing and the water rapidly rising, they could achieve no more. Phillips did not survive. Bride, however, did survive and was one of those ultimately rescued from collapsible B.

Back on the boat deck, Lightoller was organising the loading of collapsible boat

D. When this was lowered at 2.05am, there were 37 women and children on board, mostly third class, as well as three members of crew. Although Lightoller had attempted to prevent any men other than crewmen boarding, one third class passenger had smuggled himself on board and as the boat was lowered two more men leapt on board. A third man, Frederick Hoyt (whose wife was already on board the boat), also jumped but missed the boat and had to be plucked from the sea. Collapsible D, with a capacity of 47, departed with 44 crew and passengers on board.

With the bulk of the lifeboats now launched – only collapsibles A and B located on the roof of the deckhouse remained – those on board the ship were effectively resigned to their fate. In the first class smoking room a group of passengers – Archie Butt, Frank Millet, Clarence Moore and Arthur Ryerson – played cards and had a final drink before heading out on deck. The *Titanic*'s designer Thomas Andrews was last spotted staring at the painting over the fireplace in the same room. At the stern of the stricken vessel, Father Thomas Byles was offering confession whilst Wallace Hartley and the orchestra,

having played more popular music to this point, switched to playing hymns.

Elsewhere, as the water gradually encroached upon the boat deck, a number of the ship's officers and men – Wilde, Murdoch, Lightoller and Moody amongst them – were struggling to release collapsible boats A and B. The former had been snagged in the rigging and so attention was switched to the latter. There is some uncertainty as to how collapsible A reached the water – contradictory evidence was given subsequently – but it did find its way into the water the correct way up. Unfortunately, during the process the sides of the boat collapsed and, of those who tried to get aboard the boat whilst it was semi-flooded, only 14 survived to be rescued. As the rising water rushed over the roof, collapsible lifeboat B was washed overboard and ended up in the sea upside down.

By now the ship was in its death throes, with some 1,500 passengers and crew still on board. There was inevitably increasing panic, particularly amongst those from third class who had only just made their escape on to deck. By this stage both Lightoller and Bride had entered the water, with the latter

under the upturned collapsible B. Other passengers, such as Archibald Gracie and 17-year-old Jack Thayer — who had been separated from his parents earlier — also decided to take their chances in the water. Thayer swam strongly until he was some 40 yards from the ship and looked back. He commented later, 'The ship seemed to be surrounded with a glare and stood out of the night as though she were on fire.' Another witness to the final sinking, Mrs Charlotte Collyer in lifeboat No 14, recalled that the ship resembled 'an enormous glow worm, for she was alight from the rising waterline, clear to her stern… electric lights blazing in every cabin, lights on all decks, and lights on her mastheads.' With the ship's generators still producing electricity, lights were even visible from those cabins now under water, giving the sea a peculiar luminescence.

Whilst the onlookers watched, the forward funnel, already partially submerged, broke away with a minor explosion. The second funnel was also now partially inundated as those on the lifeboats heard explosions from within the ship. Finally, just after 2.15am, the ship's generators gave way, plunging the ship and all those around it into

◀ Lifeboats surround the sinking *Titanic*.

THE FINAL MOMENTS

▶ Survivors in a
lifeboat nearing
the *Carpathia*.
The arrow points
to J Bruce Ismay.

darkness. Of the *Titanic's* 34 engineering officers who had struggled to keep power going to the very end, not one deserted their post and not one was to survive. According to Lord Beresford, 'Had it not been for their steadfast dedication to duty, many more lives would have been lost.'

With the ship now virtually vertical in the water, the *Titanic* finally sank at 2.20am. At the time there was some debate as to whether the ship's back was broken before she actually sank. According to Jack Thayer, who had by now boarded the upturned collapsible B in the company of Lightoller, 'The ship did not break in two and could not be broken in two. The ship was at 60° when the lights went out, but the stern continued to rise until it was vertical.' Lightoller, Lowe and Pitman were also of the opinion that the ship sank intact, although their view was contradicted by a number of surviving crew members who expressed a belief that the ship had broken up prior to sinking, although they couldn't agree on the point where the ship did actually break its back.

At the time it was impossible to verify the nature of the actual sinking; it took the discovery of the wreck more than 70 years later to confirm that the ship had, indeed, broken up as she sank.

With the ship sunk, the survivors on board the various lifeboats were left awaiting rescue. Fifth Officer Lowe gathered together a number of lifeboats – Nos 4, 10, 12 and 14 as well as collapsible D – and, by redistributing the survivors between the various boats, he cleared No 14 of all except a small crew. It was his intention to return to the site of the sinking to pick up survivors; however, it was to be an hour before he was able to make the return and, by that time, most of those in the water had died. He was, however, to pluck five from the freezing water alive, although one of these – a steward – subsequently died.

Meanwhile, on its rescue mission the *Carpathia* was encountering icebergs. Captain Rostron later commented, 'It lay two points on the port bow and it was one whose presence was betrayed by the star beam. More and more we were all keyed up. Icebergs loomed up and fell astern; we never slackened, though sometimes we altered course suddenly to avoid them. It was an anxious time with the *Titanic's*

fateful experience very close in our minds. There were 700 souls on the *Carpathia*; these lives, as well as all the survivors of the *Titanic* itself depended on a sudden turn of the wheel.'

It was a long and cold night for those in the lifeboats until the rockets from the *Carpathia* were spotted just before dawn. As the sun started to rise over the eastern horizon, the *Carpathia* came into view. Having safely negotiated the icefield to the point where the *Titanic* was believed to have sunk, Captain Rostron ordered the engines of the *Carpathia* to be stopped whilst the crew scanned the sea for evidence of wreckage and survivors. Nothing was immediately visible. Suddenly, a crew member spotted a green light close to the water; it was a flare from lifeboat No 2 under the command of Fourth Officer Boxhall.

RMS *Carpathia* reached the site and started to pick up survivors from the lifeboats. The first person to be taken on board was first class passenger Elizabeth Allen from lifeboat No 2; she confirmed that the *Titanic* had indeed sunk. As well as the passengers, the *Carpathia* took on board most of the *Titanic*'s lifeboats, with the exception of the collapsible

boats and the leaking No 14.

Meanwhile, at around 5.15am Captain Lord ordered the engines of the *Californian* started. Spotting a vessel that he believed to be in distress, he ordered that Evans, the ship's wireless operator, be roused. Having switched on his wireless, Evans issued a 'CQ' message – 'All stations, someone answer'. He received an immediate reply from the German-owned *Frankfurt* telling him that the *Titanic* had sunk during the night at 41°46′N/50°14′W – a position that Lord estimated to be some 19.5 miles from the *Californian*'s current position.

On reaching the *Titanic*'s last known position, the *Californian* found no evidence of wreckage or survivors, but spotted the *Carpathia* to the southeast and headed towards her. Leaving the *Californian* to continue the search for survivors, the *Carpathia* departed the site of the sinking to make for New York with the survivors on board.

At 10.25am the following day, the *Californian* sent a wireless message to the *Carpathia*: 'Searched vicinity of disaster until noon yesterday, saw very little wreckage, no bodies, no sign of missing boat, regards Lord.'

◄ An illustration of the imagined fate of the *Titanic*, lying on the sea bed.

The Sinking of
the Titanic

▶ The *Caronia*,
which sent radio
messages to
the *Titanic*.

The following timeline is based upon the timings generally recorded in print after the sinking of the *Titanic*.

9.00am – Captain Barr of the *Caronia* sent a radio message to the *Titanic*: 'Captain, *Titanic* – Westbound steamers report bergs, growlers and field ice in 42° to 51°W, 12th April. Compliments – Barr.' The message was received by Captain Smith and acknowledged by him. *Titanic* was 100 miles north and 30 miles east of the position quoted. The position of the ice was noted in the chart room. This message would appear to be the only one that was received by the bridge.

1.42pm – The SS *Baltic* sent a radio message to the *Titanic*: 'Captain Smith, *Titanic* – Have had moderate variable winds and clear, fine weather since leaving. Greek steamer *Athenai* reports passing icebergs and large quantities of field ice today in lat 41°51′N, long 49°52′W... Wish you and *Titanic* all success – Commander.' *Titanic* was 45 miles north and 180 miles east of the ice, but was closing on the location at 22 knots. The message was passed to Captain Smith, who acknowledged it. At the subsequent inquiry, it was reported by one of the surviving officers that the information about ice failed to reach the bridge and was thus not plotted on the ship's charts.

1.45pm – A warning was issued by the SS *Amerika* that icebergs lay south of the *Titanic*'s intended route. As the warning had been issued to the US Hydrographic Department, the message wasn't relayed to the bridge.

5.50pm – The *Titanic* altered course from S62°W to S86°W at the 'Corner', the point at 42°N latitude where the *Titanic* was to cross the 47°W longitude.

6.00pm – Second Officer Lightoller replaced Chief Officer Wilde on watch

on the bridge, noting that *Titanic* was sailing at 'full ahead' on a course of S86°W true.

7.00pm – The outside air temperature was 43°F (6°C). The three extra boilers lit during the morning were connected to the engines, giving the ship an extra knot of speed if required.

7.15pm – Lamp Trimmer Samuel Hemmings reported to the bridge that all the ship's navigation lights were in place. First Officer Murdoch ordered him to close the fore-scuttle hatch 'as we are in the vicinity of ice and there is a glow coming from that and I want everything dark before the bridge.'

7.30pm – Bride intercepted a message from the *Californian* to SS *Antillian*: 'The Captain, *Antillian*: 6.30pm apparent ship's time; lat 42°3′N, long 49°9′W. Three large bergs five miles to southward of us. Regards – Lord.' Bride subsequently claimed that he'd taken the message to the bridge but none of the surviving officers could recall this. The outside air temperature had dropped to 39°F (4°C); the rapidly dropping temperature was evidence of the potential presence of ice. Lightoller took a star sight with his sextant in order to ascertain the ship's position. This reading was later used to estimate the ship's position when issuing the distress messages over the wireless.

8.00pm – Archie Jewell and George Symons replaced George Hogg and Frank Evans as look-outs. Officers Boxhall and Moody came on duty on the bridge.

8.10pm – Lightoller gave orders to check the water on board the ship, as he was concerned about it freezing. He also asked for a message to be passed to the chief engineer to check the fresh

water for use in the boilers, which was stored in the ship's double hull. This suggests that Lightoller was concerned that the sea temperature, as well as the air temperature, might drop below freezing.

8.30pm – A hymn singing session, attended by more than 100 passengers, commenced in the second class dining room; it would continue until after 10.00pm.

8.55pm – Captain Smith returned briefly to the bridge and retired to bed at about 9.20pm, telling Lightoller, 'If it becomes at all doubtful let me know at once; I'll be just inside.'

9.30pm – A message was received from the *Mesaba*: 'To *Titanic*: In latitude 42°N to 41°25′N, longitude 49°W to 50°30′W saw much heavy pack ice and great number large icebergs, also field ice. Weather good, clear.' Again this wasn't passed on to the bridge. Lightoller ordered Moody to take a message to the look-outs, instructing them 'to keep a sharp look out for ice, particularly small ice and growlers' and to pass the message on to the look-outs due to come on duty at 10.00pm.

10.00pm – First Officer Murdoch took over the watch from Lightoller whilst Fred Fleet and Reginald Lee took over as look-outs; Symons passed on Lightoller's warning about icebergs to his replacements. Outside temperature had dropped to 32°F (0°C).

10.30pm – With his ship approaching a large icefield, Captain Lord on board the *Californian* decided to stop for the night and ordered his sole wireless operator, Cyril Evans, to warn other ships about the proximity of ice. At about the same time *Titanic* passed the eastbound SS *Rappahannock*, exchanging signals via Morse lamp in which the captain of the *Rappahannock* reported that his rudder had been damaged by ice and that the ship 'had just passed through heavy icefield and several icebergs.' The signal was acknowledged, 'Message received. Thank you. Good night.'

11.00pm – Evans tried to pass a message from the *Californian* to the *Titanic* about the presence of ice: 'We are stopped and surrounded by ice', but Jack Phillips, trying to clear a backlog of messages caused by the earlier problem with the radio equipment, cut him off replying, 'Shut up, shut up. I am busy, I am working Cape Race.'

11.30pm – Cyril Evans switched off his radio on board the *Californian* and

retired to bed, meaning that any further wireless transmissions would be missed by the crew of the *Californian*.

11.39pm – Look-outs Fleet and Lee spotted a large iceberg. Fleet sounded the ship's bell three times and called the bridge on the telephone. He relayed the message, 'Iceberg, right ahead.' Murdoch rushed in, having seen the iceberg some 800 yards ahead, and ordered 'Hard a-starboard' and 'Stop: full speed astern.' The *Titanic* managed to turn 22.5° to port before the iceberg struck. At the same time, Murdoch pulled the lever that automatically closed the 15 watertight doors in the bulkheads.

11.40pm – The *Titanic* struck the iceberg but most people remarked on how slight the actual impact felt. Woken by the collision, Captain Smith returned to the bridge.

12 midnight – Fleet and Lee were relieved as look-outs by Hogg and Evans who remained at their post in the crow's nest until about 12.30am. The air temperature had fallen to 27°F (almost -3°C) and the sea temperature was 28°F (-2°C).

12.05am – Captain Smith ordered the uncovering of the lifeboats. The floor of the squash court on F deck, some 32 feet above the keel was awash and water was entering boiler room No 5, the sixth watertight compartment from the stern.

12.10am – Captain Smith ordered the lifeboats to be swung out ready for use. Fourth Officer Boxhall estimated the ship's position to be 41°46′N/50°14′W, based around the accurate position taken at 7.30pm and his estimation of distance travelled since then.

12.15am – The captain went to the wireless room and told the radio operators, 'You had better get assistance.' Phillips immediately started sending out the distress call 'CQD'. The first distress message was heard by the French steamer *La Provence* and by the Canadian Pacific ship *Mount Temple*. The *Mount Temple* attempted to reply but the ship's wireless was not powerful enough. The position given in the first distress call, 41°44′N/50°24′W, was incorrect.

12.18am – The *Ypiranga* picked up a distress signal; the location again being given incorrectly as 41°44′N/50°24′W. The ship received the same message 10 times.

12.25am – Captain Smith ordered that women and children be loaded on to the prepared lifeboats. At about the same time he ordered the ship's pumps into action; the failure to take this basic action earlier remains one of the most surprising aspects of the sinking. The *Carpathia* received a 'CQD' message from the *Titanic*: 'Come at once. We have struck a berg. It's a CQD, OM [Old Man] Position 41°46′N/50°14′W.' The message was also received by the land-based wireless station at Cape Race and passed on.

12.26am – A longer distress signal from the *Titanic* was heard by the *Ypiranga*: 'CQD. Here corrected position 41°46′N/50°14′W. Require immediate assistance. We have collision with iceberg. Sinking. Can hear nothing for noise of steam.' It was repeated around 15 times and followed by a further message: 'I require assistance immediately. Struck by iceberg in 41°46′N/50°14′W.'

12.30am – The *Frankfurt* received a message from the *Titanic*: 'We have collision with iceberg. Sinking. Please tell captain to come.'

12.45am – Fourth Officer Boxhall launched the first white distress rocket; the exact number of distress rockets eventually fired is uncertain, with estimates ranging from eight to more

Form No. 4.—100—17.8.10.

Deld. Date __14 APR 1912__

The Marconi International Marine Communication Co., Ltd.,
WATERGATE HOUSE, YORK BUILDINGS, ADELPHI, LONDON, W.C.

No. __"O L Y M P I C"__ .... OFFICE. ...... 14 Apr 19 12

CHARGES TO PAY.

Handed in at ___TITANIC___

This message has been transmitted subject to the conditions printed on the back hereof, which have been agreed to by the Sender. If the accuracy of this message be doubted, the Receiver, on paying the necessary charges, may have it repeated whenever possible, from Office to Office over the Company's system, and should any error be shown to exist, all charges for such repetition will be refunded. This Form must accompany any enquiry respecting this Telegram.

Total

To   OLYMPIC

Eleven pm NEW YORK TIME TITANIC SENDING OUT SIGNALS OF DISTRESS ANSWERED HIS CALLS.

TITANIC REPLIES AND GIVES ME HIS POSITION 41.46 N 50 14 W AND SAYS "WE HAVE STRUCK AN ICE BERG".

OUR DISTANCE FROM TITANIC 505 MILES.

than 20. Lifeboat No 7, with only 28 people on board, was the first to be launched. Lightoller ordered all women and children to descend to A deck to board the lifeboats from that level but the windows on A deck were locked. Lightoller ordered that the key be found.

Phillips issued his first 'SOS' message to the *Olympic*, which was then some 500 nautical miles away.

12.50am – *Titanic* radioed: 'I require immediate assistance. Position 41°46′N/50°14′W' – a message received by the *Celtic*.

12.55am – Lifeboat No 5 was launched with 39 passengers and crew on board and a further two male passengers who leapt aboard as it was being lowered.

12.55am – Port-side lifeboat No 6 was launched, occupied by 24 women, two crew, one male passenger with yachting experience and a male stowaway. Whilst at sea, lifeboat No 6 picked up another crew member, a stoker.

1.00am – Lifeboat No 3 was launched with some 14 women and children, 12 male passengers and up to 14 members of crew, making a possible 38 to 40 in all.

1.02am – The *Titanic* sent a message to the *Asian* requesting assistance.

1.10am – Lifeboat No 1 was launched. On board this lifeboat designed to hold 40 were just 12 people. At the same time lifeboat No 8 was launched with 24 passengers and four members of crew on board. A further message was sent from the *Titanic* to the *Olympic*: 'We are in collision with berg. Sinking, head down. Come as soon as possible. Get your boats ready.'

1.20am – Lifeboat No 9 was launched with 56 on board, including

at least nine male passengers and 15 crew. Also launched was lifeboat No 10 with 55 on board, including four members of crew to handle the boat once it hit the water.

1.25am – Lifeboat No 11 was launched – with about 70 on board – and the last distress rocket was fired. This was followed by lifeboat No 12, with 43 passengers and crew, and No 14 with up to 64 on board – the latter springing a leak as it dropped into the water after having had to be released manually. A third message from the *Titanic* to the *Olympic* was picked up by the *Carpathia*: 'We are putting the women off in the small boats.'

1.35am – Lifeboat No 16 was lowered with 56 passengers and crew on board. Meanwhile lifeboat No 13 was lowered from the starboard side with around 64 on board and, as it drifted, was nearly crushed by lifeboat No 15 being lowered from above with 68 or 70 aboard. A further message was sent from the *Titanic*: 'Engine room getting flooded.'

1.40am – Collapsible lifeboat C, with 39-44 people on board was lowered. Cape Race sent a message to the *Virginian*: 'Please tell your Captain this: The *Olympic* is making all speed for

Titanic, but his [the *Olympic's*] position is 40°32′N/61°18′W. You are much nearer to *Titanic*. The *Titanic* is already putting women off in the boats, and he says the weather there is calm and clear. The *Olympic* is the only ship we have heard say, "Going to the assistance of the *Titanic*." The others must be a long way from the *Titanic*.' The last distress rocket was fired from the *Titanic*.

1.45am – Lifeboat No 2 was lowered with 25 on board. A final message was picked up by the *Carpathia*: 'Engine room full up to boilers.' The wireless room log on board the *Carpathia* recorded that at '12.20am [2.10am *Titanic* time] Signals were broken.'

1.47am – The *Caronia* heard a message from the *Titanic*, but the signal was weak and couldn't be read.

1.48am – The *Asian* heard an 'SOS' from the *Titanic* but couldn't get a response to its reply.

1.50am – The *Caronia* heard transmissions between the *Frankfurt* and the *Titanic*; this was the last message that the *Caronia* heard transmitted from the latter.

1.55am – Lifeboat No 4 was launched with around 40 people on board. Cape Race sent a message to the

Virginian: 'We have not heard *Titanic* for about half an hour. His power may be gone.'

2.00am – The rising water reached the forward boat deck. The *Virginian* heard a faint signal from the *Titanic* but nothing further.

2.05am – The water had now reached the bottom of the bridge rail and the ship's propellers were rising out of the water. Collapsible lifeboat D was lowered with 44 people aboard. At about the same time Captain Smith relieved Bride and Phillips from their duty in the wireless room.

2.10am – Sea water swept over the forward end of the boat deck, freeing collapsible lifeboat B and washing it overboard. Collapsible lifeboat A was also launched but semi-flooded and a number of survivors clambered aboard, but no more than 14 survived to be rescued by the *Carpathia*.

2.17am – Captain Smith was allegedly sighted entering the bridge for the last time.

2.18am – The ship's electrical system finally failed.

2.20am – The *Titanic* finally sank, breaking its back between the third and fourth funnels. The stern section

remains afloat a few moments longer than the bow section.

2.45am – The Second Officer on the *Carpathia*, James Bisset, spotted the first of several icebergs.

3.30am – The rockets from the

RMS *Carpathia* were first spotted by the survivors in the lifeboats.

4.00am – The *Carpathia* spotted a flare from lifeboat No 2.

4.10am – The first of the survivors were taken on board the *Carpathia* from lifeboat No 2, followed by those from lifeboat No 7.

4.30am – Captain Lord on the *Californian* was awakened by George V Stewart, the officer of the watch.

4.45am – Lifeboat No 13 was the eighth or ninth to come alongside the *Carpathia* and the passengers were taken aboard.

5.15am – Captain Lord of the *Californian* ordered the ship southwards to make for the *Titanic's* last known position at top speed (13.5 knots), having learned of its fate from the *Frankfurt*.

6.00am – Lifeboat No 3 came alongside the *Carpathia* and its passengers were taken aboard.

6.15am – The passengers from collapsible lifeboat C were picked up by the *Carpathia*.

6.30am – Having carefully made progress through the icefield, the *Californian* reached open water. The survivors on board the upturned

collapsible B were picked up by lifeboat No 12, meaning that this boat was now offering accommodation for some 70 passengers and crew under the command of Lightoller.

7.00am – Lifeboat 14, under the command of Fifth Officer Lowe, towing collapsible lifeboat D went alongside the *Carpathia*.

7.30am – The *Californian* reached the point recorded as being the *Titanic's* last known position and, finding no evidence of wreckage or survivors, headed for the *Carpathia*, spotted to the southeast.

8.00am – Lifeboat No 6, under the command of Quartermaster Robert Hichens came alongside the *Carpathia*.

8.30am – The final lifeboat to be picked up – the overloaded lifeboat No 12 under the command of Second Officer Lightoller – was pulled alongside the *Carpathia*. Shortly afterwards, the *Californian* arrived alongside at 41°33′N/50°01′W.

8.50am – The *Carpathia* departed to make for New York with the survivors on board.

10.30am – Having searched the area of the sinking, the *Californian* resumed its trip to Boston.

◀ Survivors of the disaster gathered after rescue.

Aftermath

Following the sinking, and the recovery of the survivors, a total of around 705 were found to have survived the sinking, although the exact figure is unknown. The number of fatalities is also uncertain, but the total is generally thought to be between 1,502 and 1,523, making it the worst sea disaster to have occurred up to that point in history.

Having departed from the scene of the sinking later on the morning of 15 April, the *Carpathia* arrived at New York during the evening of 18 April at about 9.35pm. After depositing the *Titanic*'s lifeboats at Pier 59, as these were the property of White Star Line, the *Carpathia* docked at Pier 54. Vast crowds witnessed the survivors disembarking from the *Carpathia*.

In order to assist, the US Immigration Service allowed all the passengers, irrespective of class, immediate access to land; normally, those seeking immigration into the country would have been transferred to Ellis Island for processing, but on this occasion the examination was waived. The last people to be transferred from the *Carpathia* were the surviving members of the crew. They were taken to accommodation on board the Red Star Line's *Lapland*.

In order to recover the bodies, White Star Line chartered the cable ship CS *Mackay-Bennett* from Halifax, Nova Scotia, and this ship with three others – the *Minia* (another cable ship), *Montmagny* (a lighthouse supply ship belonging to the Canadian Ministry of Marine and Fisheries) and *Algerine* (a sealing vessel) – recovered 328 bodies. A further five were recovered by passing steamships. Of the 333 bodies recovered, 124 were buried at sea with the remainder being returned to Halifax, where the local coroner exercised jurisdiction. A total of 59 bodies were reclaimed by family members and transported to the USA or back to Britain for burial and the remaining 150 were buried in the three cemeteries in Halifax, with burials commencing on 3 May 1912. Of the bodies recovered, 128 remained unidentified despite the best efforts of the crews of the recovery ships in trying to ensure that all evidence of identity was secured.

One unidentified body was to affect the crew of the *Mackay-Bennett* profoundly. This was the body of a two-year-old boy. When it came to the child's burial, Captain Lardner of the *Mackay-Bennett* and his crew paid for the service and for a gravestone. More recent research has suggested that the child was one of a Scandinavian migrant family and that, if the tentative identification is correct, he is buried close to the grave of his mother.

With such a loss of life, it was inevitable that inquiries would be held into the causes of the accident and the lessons that could be learnt from it. The American Inquiry was chaired by Senator William Alden Smith and formally opened on 19 April, although the initial work had been undertaken on the *Carpathia* when it docked on 18 April and when Smith first interviewed J Bruce Ismay.

William Alden Smith, a Republican

THE BRIEF CAREER OF THE LARGEST LINER
DESCRIBED IN THREE TABLEAUX

Senator from Michigan, headed a six-man commission, formed of three Democrats and three Republicans, which sat for 17 days between 19 April

and 25 May in the Waldorf–Astoria Hotel in New York. He was a lawyer, builder and railway operator but was characterised in the US press as being something of a fool. This may have been because he was from the mid-west rather than from the more sophisticated east coast. He was conscious that under the terms of the 1898 Harter Act shipping lines could be sued in the event of an accident if negligence could be proved. He was, however, highly objective in his work and in his ultimate report.

During the course of his inquiry, Smith interviewed a total of 82 witnesses, comprising 53 British and 29 US citizens. Of these, two were officers from International Mercantile Marine, four were the surviving officers from the *Titanic* itself, 34 were members of the ship's crew and 21 were passengers (with representatives from all three classes). There were a total of 1,145 pages of testimony and Smith's report extended to some 19 pages with a further 44 pages of evidence. The cost of the US Inquiry was around $6,600.

Smith came up with two main recommendations, both of which were swiftly converted into legislation. The first concerned lifeboats and the

necessity both of providing sufficient numbers for all passengers and crew and that adequate training in their use needed to be given. The second recommendation related to the use of radios and the need to ensure that all ships kept them manned 24 hours a day with adequate power supply and action to prevent interference.

The *Lapland* set sail on 20 April without 34 of the surviving members of the *Titanic*'s crew and the four surviving officers, who had to remain in New York to ensure that relevant members of the ship's crew were available to assist the US Inquiry. The ship reached Plymouth at around 7.00am on 29 April, but despite the presence of a vast crowd of family members, press and others, the survivors were not immediately allowed to depart, as representatives of the Board of Trade were determined to try to interview them. Initially, the crew were reluctant to answer questions but, with the arrival of their union representatives, this process began and later that day and the next, the British survivors were finally allowed to make their way home.

A week later, on 6 May, the *Celtic* docked at Liverpool; on board was

◀ A boy selling newspapers with the dreaded headline, no one expected to hear.

AFTERMATH

a further batch of crew members, including look-outs Fleet and Lee. The body of bandleader Wallace Hartley arrived back in Liverpool on board the *Arabic* on 12 May and on 18 May wireless operator Harold Bride arrived back at Liverpool on board the *Baltic*. Three days later the *Adriatic* arrived at the port with Ismay on board in the company of Officers Lightoller, Lowe and Pitman.

The British Inquiry, chaired by the Wreck Commissioner of the Board of Trade, John Charles Bigham (Lord Mersey), was held between 2 May and 3 July. The building selected for the inquiry was the Drill Hall of the London Scottish Regiment, which was located close to Buckingham Palace. Whilst this was a large building, capable of holding several hundred people (as interest from the press and public was expected to be great), the acoustics left much to be desired. The inquiry set itself the task of answering 26 questions covering the construction and state of the ship as she sailed from Southampton, the journey across the Atlantic and the warnings received, the damage received by the ship and the actual sinking, and how those who

survived were rescued. During the course of the inquiry, a further question on the role of Captain Lord and the *Californian* was also considered.

In order to aid the deliberations of Lord Mersey and his assessors, a 20-foot model of the *Titanic* – like the original, built by Harland & Wolff – was displayed behind the witness box. Also visible were a large plan of the North Atlantic and a 40-foot-long side plan of the ship, the latter designed to illustrate the complexity of the ship in terms of possible evacuation.

The Board of Trade was represented at the inquiry by the Attorney General, Sir Rufus Isaacs KC, who was assisted by the Solicitor General, Sir John Simon. It was the latter who raised the initial list of questions that the inquiry was designed to try to answer. White Star Line was represented by the Right Honourable Sir Robert Finlay KC MP, whilst the National Sailors' & Firemen's Union was represented, on the instructions of Captain Smith's widow, by Thomas Scanlan MP. A number of other parties were, however, denied representation; these included Captain Lord and the *Californian*, whose representative was allowed only to act

▲ Survivors of the disaster being awarded shipwreck pay by the National Sailors and Firemen's Union.

as an observer and could not have any direct role in the inquiry.

Following opening submissions, the inquiry team travelled to Southampton on 6 May 1912 in order to see for themselves the *Olympic*, which had been made available for the inspection. Back at the Drill Hall, the inquiry

examined people involved in the disaster itself, both crew and survivors, as well as noted experts such as the famous Antarctic explorer Sir Ernest Shackleton. Captain Lord himself gave evidence on the seventh day of the inquiry. Other members of the crew of the *Californian* were also interviewed, as were Captain Rostron and the crew of the *Carpathia*. By 21 June, when the taking of testimony ceased, a total of 25,622 questions had been asked and answered. Following a further eight days of summations and closing arguments, the inquiry adjourned to allow Lord Mersey to complete his report. He presented his conclusions at the end of July 1912. Amongst his many comments were three and a half pages criticising Captain Lord and the failure of the *Californian* to make greater efforts to reach the stricken ship.

The British Inquiry concluded that 'the loss of the said ship was due to collision with an iceberg brought on by the excessive speed at which the ship was being navigated.' It had been claimed, although the evidence for this was limited and disputed by many, that J Bruce Ismay had encouraged Captain Smith to push the *Titanic* to the maximum, and clearly the British Inquiry was of the opinion that given the prevailing conditions, the captain should have been more cautious.

Following both inquiries, a number of changes were made to maritime practice, ship design and operation, all aimed at ensuring that a similar tragedy could not recur in future. On 12 November 1913 the first International Convention for the Safety of Life at Sea was convened in London. On 30 January 1914 a treaty was signed that led to the creation and funding of the International Ice Patrol. As part of the United States Coast Guard, this continues in operation to the present day and is tasked with monitoring and reporting all icebergs identified in the North Atlantic that might pose a threat to transatlantic shipping. Ship designs were modified to incorporate deeper bulkheads and the use of double-hull technology. Reflecting the conclusions of the British Inquiry, the Board of Trade in London introduced regulations instructing captains to reduce speed if there was any likelihood of

▲ Lord Mersey, John Charles Bigham who presided over the British Inquiry.

meeting icebergs.

Of all the consequences of the sinking of the *Titanic*, the most significant was perhaps to prove as fallacious the historic belief that it was not necessary to provide sufficient lifeboats to hold all passengers and crew as those available would be adequate to ferry people from the stricken vessel to one of the many other vessels that would have responded to the distress signals.

The question of litigation and compensation followed on the heels of the two inquiries. Under the terms of the Merchant Ships Act, White Star Line was liable for the freight lost – a sum of £123,711 – but there were also claims lodged in US courts for personal losses of lives and goods amounting to $16,804,112. The company took action to limit its liabilities under American law and the case was heard by the United States District Court, Southern District of New York. The claims for loss of property extended from William Carter's Renault 35hp

car (valued at $5,000) to a copy of the
magazine *Science & Health* for which
Annie May Stengel claimed $5.00.
Legal action in both the USA and UK
dragged on until, in late 1915, lawyers
for both parties reached the outline of
a settlement. This was concluded on 28
July 1916, when Judge Julius M Mayer
signed a decree terminating all law suits.
A total of $663,000 was distributed
amongst the individual claimants
following this agreement.

▲ Sir Rufus
Isaacs KC.

◄ Sir John
Simon who
assisted Sir
Rufus Isaacs.

Discovery

Almost from the moment that the *Titanic* sank there had been efforts to track the ship down, although some of the proposals to attempt to salvage the vessel were perhaps farfetched. Early searches for the wreck were hampered by the fact that the last position reported by the ship – 41°46′N/50°14′W – was some 13 nautical miles from the actual location at 41°43′55″N/49°56′45″W where the ship was ultimately discovered.

It was not until 1 September 1985 that a joint US-French survey, funded in part by the National Geographic Society and by French taxpayers, on the research vessel *Knorr* finally made the breakthrough. Using a remotely-controlled camera on board an unmanned submersible, *Argo*, the wreck was discovered to the southeast of Newfoundland at a depth of 12,000 feet. The discovery represented the culmination of almost two months of investigation.

The 1985 expedition was led by Dr Robert Ballard and Dr Nicholas S E Cappon of the Woods Hole Oceanographic Institution and Jean-Louis Michel of Ifremer (Institut Français de recherche pour l'exploitation de la mer – the French institute for exploitation of the sea). The French vessel *Le Surôit* sailed on 1 July 1985 for the wreck site, reaching the area on 9 July. For 10 days, using sonar scans 3,000 feet wide, the ship criss-crossed the North Atlantic searching for the wreck. Finding nothing, the ship sailed to the French territory of St Pierre et Miquelon, just to the south of Newfoundland, for refuelling on 19 July. Whilst there, the French crew was joined by Robert Ballard and other members of the Woods Hole team prior to sailing once more to the wreck site.

A further search of the supposed area of the wreck resumed on 26 July but, with 80% of the area surveyed by early August, time was running out for this phase of the search as *Le Surôit* was required for other duties elsewhere. With the French ship withdrawn from the search, Dr Ballard and other scientists flew to the Azores where they joined the Woods Hole survey vessel, *Knorr*. Loaded on board the ship were the two submersibles – *Argo*, a deep-towed undersea video camera sled and *Angus*, a deep-towed underwater still camera sled – which would prove essential in diving down to the depth of almost two and a half miles where the wreck was

ultimately located. The *Knorr* sailed from the Azores on 17 August but, before heading for the site of the *Titanic*, the crew diverted to survey the wreck of the USS *Scorpion,* a nuclear submarine that had been lost with all hands in 1968, which they located using a debris field.

The *Knorr* reached the *Titanic* search area on 22 August 1985 and *Argo* began sweeping back and forth just above the ocean floor. Ballard's team took shifts monitoring the video feed, looking for signs on the smooth seabed of the debris field that would have formed after implosions due to pressure differences inside and outside the ship as it sank over two miles to the ocean floor below. Finally, in the early morning of 1 September, observers noted pockmarks, like small craters from impacts, and eventually debris was sighted. At last, a boiler came into view and, soon after, the hull itself was found.

As *Knorr* was required for other duties, there was time only for a general survey of the *Titanic*'s exterior. On their return to North America, Ballard and his team held a press conference, concluding, 'It is quiet and peaceful and a fitting place for the remains of this greatest of sea tragedies to rest. May it

forever remain that way and may God bless these found souls.'

The imagery recorded by the *Argo*'s camera showed that the *Titanic* had broken in two, with the bow and the badly damaged stern sections separated by a distance of some 650 yards and a considerable debris field surrounding it. Although the non-ferrous items on the ship were reasonably well preserved, all organic material – including bodies – had disappeared and the iron was encrusted with rust. The state of the ship and the depth at which she lay precluded any possibility of the wreck being raised.

Once the *Titanic* had been discovered, it was inevitable that interest in the ship would increase dramatically. Further exploration of the site has followed and, with advances in underwater photography and filming, stunning images of the wreck have emerged.

Once the wreck was discovered there was a considerable debate as to who actually owned the wreck and the artefacts on board, and ownership has been subject to legal dispute on both sides of the Atlantic. There has also been legislation to try to ensure that the site of the wreck is treated as a grave for those who perished, as are the sites of

◄ A portion of the first class C deck.

DISCOVERY

warships sunk in battle.

Following legal action in the USA, RMS Titanic Inc – a subsidiary of Premier Exhibitions Inc – was granted salvor-in-possession rights to the ship by a US Federal Court in 1994, a decision that was confirmed by a second ruling in 1996. However, although granted salvage rights, the company was not granted ownership of the artefacts retrieved. A ruling in August 2010 stated that RMS Titanic Inc is entitled to the full market value of the artefacts displayed, but the decision on whether to sell the artefacts through the court or to give the company title to the objects after setting conditions for their maintenance and future use may not be made until August 2011. The company has undertaken seven expeditions – in 1987, 1993, 1994, 1996, 1998, 2000 and 2004 – to recover artefacts from the ship. In the late summer of 2010, a joint expedition with scientists from the Woods Hole Oceanographic Institution visited the wreck site and used imaging devices and sonar data to create a detailed 3-D map of the wreck and debris field. No artefacts were recovered on this trip.

To date some 5,500 objects in all have been raised, ranging from a 17-ton section of the bow to a child's marble. After many years submerged at a depth of over two miles and subjected to vast pressure and the impact of corrosion and chemical action, all of the items recovered have had to be carefully conserved prior to display.

These artefacts, along with documentation, form the basis of a travelling exhibition – *Titanic*: The Artifact Exhibition – that has so far been seen by some 18 million people in various parts of the world. The exhibition was brought to the National Maritime Museum in Greenwich during 1994 and 1995, although not without controversy – largely as a result of concerns about material raised from an internationally recognised grave – but it proved to be the most successful exhibition the museum had held. The exhibition also came to Manchester in 2005.

Whilst individual items recovered from the *Titanic* can be conserved, the greatest relic of them all – the remains of the ship itself – is much more vulnerable. The discovery of the ship, subsequent voyages by remote cameras and, more recently, by submersibles capable of taking people down to the wreck, as well as efforts to try to salvage parts from the debris field and the ship, have accelerated

the process of disintegration. The threat was recognised by Robert Ballard himself when he wrote in his book, *The Discovery of the Titanic* (published in 1987): 'For now the greatest threat to the *Titanic* clearly comes from man, in the form of crude dredging operations.'

The Titanic Myths

▶ *Titanic*
in the dock.

Almost from the point at which the ship sank, the *Titanic* has been the subject of various conspiracy theories and supposed curses. Amongst the various myths and legends that have sprung up over the years are the following – the majority of which are completely fallacious:

• That several Catholic workers at Harland & Wolff – a company noted historically for its strong bias towards Protestant employees – walked out as a result of anti-Catholic slogans painted on board; this graffiti was noted by crew members at Queenstown. One of the Catholics who walked off was alleged to have said, 'This ship will not finish its first voyage.'

• That the construction of the ship was so rapid that at least one worker was sealed up in the hull and left to die. In fact, the number of casualties during the construction of the *Titanic* was lower than the one per £100,000 value of the contract that was the accepted norm at the time. Only two fatalities

are known to have occurred during the construction of the ship.

• That the hull number 390904, when shown in a mirror, can be read as 'NO POPE', and is therefore practically blasphemous and certainly unlucky.

• That a cursed Egyptian mummy was on board, which inspired the sinking of the ship in order to exact revenge on its owner. There is no record of the supposed mummy in the manifest of cargo taken on board the ship. However, during the voyage journalist William T Stead – a noted spiritualist (as were many influential people at the time) – told guests at a dinner party about a mummy then on display in the British Museum. This may be the origin of the story.

• That the bottle of champagne used when the ship was christened at launching failed to break. Believed to be an indication of bad luck, this was unlikely to have happened with the *Titanic* as normal White Star Line policy was not to christen its ships when they were launched.

• That the notoriously parochial Aberdeen *Press and Journal* recorded the sinking under the headline 'Aberdeenshire Man Drowned at Sea'. The actual headline used was 'Mid-Atlantic Disaster: *Titanic* Sunk by Iceberg'. There were several other variations on this theme; all are equally fanciful.

• That there was a mystery ship present close to the *Titanic*. Fourth Officer Joseph Boxhall believed that he'd seen the lights of a second vessel shortly after midnight and other members of the crew subsequently reported seeing lights as well. In addition, Colonel Gracie and other passengers also believed that they saw a second ship's lights. At the subsequent British Inquiry, this vessel was identified as the *Californian* and thus led to considerable bad feeling towards Captain Lord. Subsequent inquiries, particularly since the discovery of the wreck, have cast some doubt on this, although the official position remains equivocal about the actual location of the *Californian* in relation to the sinking.

• That a large number of prominent passengers cancelled at the last moment with premonitions of disaster. A certain

number undoubtedly did cancel, but most of these were for more prosaic reasons. An American steel baron, Henry Frick and his wife were booked to travel; however, Mrs Frick sprained her ankle whilst on Madeira; their booking was taken over by financier and International Mercantile Marine owner J P Morgan, who also cancelled – the reasons cited vary from his being unwell to over-running business negotiations to visiting his French mistress. This ill-fated booking was then taken over by another American businessman, J Horace Harding, who transferred to the *Mauretania*. The ex-US ambassador to France, Robert Bacon, was also scheduled to travel on the *Titanic* with his wife; however, the delayed arrival of his successor meant that he had to remain in France until after the ship had sailed. George

Vanderbilt and his wife did cancel at the last minute, but this was more to do with his mother-in-law's dislike of maiden voyages. (Vanderbilt's servant, Frederick Wheeler, did travel on the ship as a second class passenger, and died in the tragedy). In all, some 55 bookings were cancelled. There was, however, at least one premonition: a Mr and Mrs E W Bill from Philadelphia transferred to the *Celtic* as a result of a dream Mrs Bill had whilst staying in a London hotel shortly before their departure. There was an added complication in the travel plans of many potential passengers, as Britain was in the midst of a coal strike and White Star Line had been forced to try to obtain coal from a variety of sources; lack of coal meant that a number of other services were cancelled or delayed with inevitable confusion for potential passengers.

• That the *Titanic* and *Olympic* were switched during the second occasion on which both were in dry dock in Belfast following the loss of the *Olympic*'s propeller. The argument here is that as a result of the *Olympic*'s collision with HMS *Hawke*, the condition of the White Star liner was much worse than generally accepted and as a result

the company would find it difficult to obtain insurance cover for the ship. The switch was arranged so that the compromised *Olympic* would sail as the brand new, and therefore easily insured, *Titanic* and when insurance assessors came to look at the *Olympic* (ex-*Titanic*), they would see a ship for which insurance could easily be given.

The Titanic in Popular Culture

▶ Actors prepare to film a lifeboat scene in the movie *A Night to Remember*.

▼ A postage stamp celebrating the release of the film *Titanic*.

The first books to feature the sinking of the *Titanic* – written by Lawrence Beesley and Archibald Gracie – appeared within months of the ship's demise and the first film, written and starring *Titanic* survivor Dorothy Gibson, also appeared during 1912. Since then, a great deal about the ship has appeared in both fact and fiction.

Films about the *Titanic* include the following:

• *Saved from the Titanic* – The original silent film starring Dorothy Gibson was released in May 1912, with prints being sent to the UK and France as well as being distributed in the USA. It was hugely successful. Unfortunately, there is no known print of this film in existence and it is therefore considered to be 'lost'. It's widely regarded as one of the greatest missing films of the silent era. Of all the films made by Dorothy Gibson, only one is known to have survived and that is *A Lucky Holdup* (1912), located and rescued in 2001.

• *A Night to Remember* – Released in 1958, this was based on Walter Lord's bestselling book of the same name, which had been published three years earlier. Directed by Roy Baker and with a screenplay by the noted thriller writer Eric Ambler, the film's stars included Kenneth More, David McCallum and Honor Blackman. Much of the film was shot at Pinewood Studios with the scenes in the water filmed at the nearby Ruislip Lido.

33 USA

A JAMES CAMERON FILM

TITANIC

Blockbuster Film

2000

THE TITANIC IN POPULAR CULTURE

• *Raise the Titanic* – Sir Lew Grade's multi-million-pound epic was released in 1980. Based on the novel of the same name by Clive Cussler, the film was directed by Jerry Jameson and the cast included Jason Robards and Sir Alec Guinness. The plot revolved around the alleged presence on board the ship of 'byzanium', a material that is required to power a defence project. The highpoint of a lacklustre film is when the liner suddenly re-emerges above the waterline. Commenting on the cost of the film, Grade stated that it would probably have been cheaper to have lowered the Atlantic.

• *Titanic* – Released in 1997 and starring Leonardo DiCaprio and Kate Winslet, this James Cameron directed film remained the highest grossing film in the history of film-making until 2010 when it was overtaken by another James Cameron offering, *Avatar*. *Titanic* cost $200 million to make and ended up winning 11 Academy Awards.

• *Ghosts of the Abyss* – This is a stunning 3D IMAX documentary filmed by James Cameron and released in 2003. The film was shot using specially created cameras that were able to get closer to the wreck than ever before and actually traverse the interior of the ship itself. Using CGI (computer-generated imagery) technology, the film recreates how the ship looked when new. Cameron was joined in the filming and narration by the actor Bill Paxton, who played the role of Brock Lovett (a fictional character) in Cameron's 1997 blockbuster.

A large number of books about the *Titanic* have been produced over the years. The first books to appear were those compiled by survivors Lawrence Beesley (1912) – *The Loss of the SS Titanic* – and Archibald Gracie (1913) – *The Truth about the Titanic*. Also published shortly after the actual tragedy were the official reports of both the British and US inquiries. It was in 1956 that the classic account, *A Night to Remember* written by Walter Lord, was first released and, with the discovery of the wreck itself, the number of books produced has grown significantly. A number of these – such as Dr Robert Ballard's *The Discovery of the Titanic* (1987) – include images taken of the wreck site itself. More recent books, such as *Titanic: Destination Disaster – The Legends and the Reality* (1987, rev 1996) – include photographs of some of the artefacts recovered from the site. There are also books devoted to the conspiracy theories, most notably *The Riddle of the Titanic* by Robin Gardiner and Dan van der Vat (1996) and Robin Gardiner's *Titanic: The Ship that Never Sank?* (2008).

As might also be expected, in the age of the internet, there are countless websites devoted to the subject. The most comprehensive is perhaps www.encyclopedia-titanica.org. This site includes information on all passengers and crew members, identifying those who survived and those who died, along with potted biographies. It also includes a vast array of references to other sources, a search facility and a message board. The Titanic Inquiry Project website at www.titanicinquiry.org contains electronic copies of the British and US inquiries into the disaster.

Titanic in Retrospect

As the centenary of the sinking of the *Titanic* approaches in 2012, plans are underway all over the world to commemorate the tragic loss of RMS *Titanic* and over 1,500 lives on 15 April 1912. The story is now passing from living history to true history, with the death of the final survivor, Millvina Dean, on 31 May 2009 and the reduction in number of those who were alive at the time. So, what will remain of the *Titanic*?

There will be the physical monuments constructed to those who lost their lives in the sinking. These include the statue raised to bandleader Wallace Hartley in Colne, Lancashire, the 'below decks' memorial now located at Holy Rood Church, Southampton, the monument raised to the ship's engineers dedicated in 1914 in the public gardens in Southampton, and the memorial constructed near Belfast City Hall, not far from where the ship was built.

There will be the various artefacts that have been brought to the surface or acquired from survivors. A new museum under development in Southampton will allow visitors to experience life on board during the ill-fated voyage from the perspective of the crew, many of whom were from the city.

There will be the wreck itself,

although the continuing deterioration of the remains and the degradation of the site caused by the presence of human activity over the past 25 years means that the wreck itself will gradually be lost forever.

There are the countless photographs – some taken whilst the ship was afloat, others since the wreck was rediscovered – that will provide a constant reminder of the splendour of the ship itself. There are also the representations, in fact and in fiction, in film and in books that will entertain and educate.

And there is the myth: the tragic story of a ship believed to be practically unsinkable that was lost with more than 1,500 lives on a cold April night in 1912.

Glossary

aft – towards the stern of the vessel

amidships/midships – in the middle portion of the ship, along the line of the keel

beam – the width of a vessel at the widest point

bow – the front of a ship

bulkhead – an upright, often watertight and load-bearing wall within the hull of a ship

davit – a device for hoisting and lowering a boat

displacement – the weight of water displaced by the ship's hull

draught/draft – the depth of a ship's keel below the waterline

fore/forward – towards the bow of the vessel

Gross Registered Tonnage – total internal volume of a vessel, where a register ton is equal to a volume of 100 cubic feet

port – towards the left-hand side of a vessel facing forward

starboard – towards the right-hand side of a vessel facing forward

stern – the rear part of a ship

To download our latest catalogue and to view
the full range of books and DVDs visit:

www.G2ent.co.uk

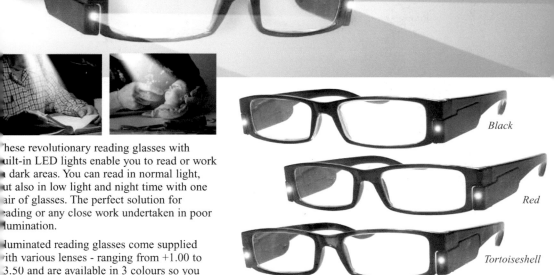

**The pictures in this book were
provided courtesy of the following:**

GETTY IMAGES
101 Bayham Street, London NW1 0AG

Design and artwork by David Wildish

Published by G2 Entertainment Limited

Publishers Jules Gammond and Alan Jones

Revised by Sue Todd